TABLE OF CONTENTS

CHAPTER 1
INTRODUCTION

"In any problem where an opposing force exists and cannot be regulated, one must foresee and provide for alternative courses. Adaptability is the law which governs survival in war as in life ..."
Sir B.H. Lidell Hart

As the counterinsurgency fight in Afghanistan approaches a decade, there are still no overwhelming signs that the International Security Forces – Afghanistan (ISAF), or the government of President Harmid Karzai are closing in on victory over insurgent Taliban forces. Despite thousands of Taliban, Afghan and Coalition casualties, an untold amount of international aid and a rigorous and ongoing effort to train both the Afghan military and police forces, Afghanistan is far from stable. In fact, insurgent activity in the wake of President Obama's troop increase is conversely on the rise. 2010 has been the deadliest year for United States troops since the war began with 499 killed while the last portions of the thirty thousand troop increase have only just arrived.[1] This is an ominous indicator that elements of our counterinsurgency (COIN) doctrine and strategy need immediate revision. Similarly, several of the assumptions that the Obama Administration has relied on to fight the insurgency in Afghanistan have come under attack due to their foundation in classic COIN theory. Regardless, Afghanistan in many ways offers the premier challenge in the study of COIN because of its geographic isolation and large size, the complex and closed nature of its culture, its traditional aversion to central government, and the ever-present influence of interlopers.

The thesis of this paper is that the nation's counterinsurgency doctrine is currently inadequate for the realities of the complex security environment that exist today and that

---

[1] ICasualties, Operation Enduring Freedom, "Coalition Military Fatalities By Year," http://icasualties.org/oef, (assessed on 2 January, 2011).

1

the U.S. must be prepared to make some major adjustments to the current counterinsurgency (COIN) doctrine as well as to the expected outcomes of future COIN campaigns. Specifically, the Services need to take into account the unique and evolving security environment faced in Afghanistan and better understand the culture and ideology that allows this unique type of global insurgency to thrive. Likewise, the government needs to better understand at the strategic level when and how to support a counterinsurgency that we deem is vital to U.S. national interests. This paper will detail the unique and emerging Afghan security environment in order to highlight why the COIN doctrine being applied is not supporting our strategic interests. Next, several recommendations and revisions are offered to improve our current COIN doctrine in order to meet U.S. objectives in Afghanistan. The suggested adaptations will be broad-spectrum and can also be applied elsewhere in the world as required.

To validate these recommended revisions and test their future applicability this paper will examine the current situation in Afghanistan and the potential for a future COIN operation in Somalia as case studies. Somalia's growing insurgency provides an excellent example of another religiously inspired revolution in a failed nation-state whose insurgent leaders share transnational terror connections with Al Qaeda. Somali insurgents already represent a threat to U.S. interests and national security, so it is critical that the U.S. military is capable of eliminating this threat more effectively than it has done in Afghanistan.

The foundational document of our current doctrine is Army Field Manual (FM) 3-24, and Marine Corps Warfighting Publication (MCWP) 3-33.5.[2] Released in December

---

[2] Army FM 3-24 and Marine Corps Warfighting Publication 3-33.5 is a single joint document that will be henceforth referred to as FM 3-24 for simplicity.

2006, it remains useful as a point of departure to rethink and revise current COIN doctrine and thereby adhere to one of the most important and enduring principles that the current document does promote: adaptability. We have learned much in the five years since the publication of FM 3-24 from both Iraq and Afghanistan. While some of the classical principles will remain, many will not and the overarching idea that the people are the prize and always the center of gravity in a COIN struggle is something that will require incessant reexamination. The problem with this paradigm is that it assumes a center of gravity for insurgents and for counterinsurgent forces will always be the people. On the other hand, esteemed military theorists such as Carl von Clausewitz prescribe that the center of gravity must be discovered for each conflict and that it may vary depending on the objectives of the war being fought.[3] This is just one of the faulty assumptions that provide a basis to challenge some of the classical theory about COIN warfare and how it is applied to both current and future insurgencies. Several critiques of current COIN doctrine will be evaluated and compared with the popular support the FM 3-24 currently receives from noted experts including Tom Ricks, David Kilcullen and John Nagl.

Many additional counterinsurgency lessons have been compiled by U.S. forces since the publication of FM 3-24 and those with merit need to be included in this recommended revision. Furthermore, the uniquely difficult counterinsurgency struggle ongoing in Afghanistan provides an excellent case study to explore what can be done to improve the ability to win against contemporary insurgents. More importantly for ISAF and the Afghan people, adapting current COIN doctrine and practice has the potential to achieve sustainable stability in Afghanistan. While the nation continues to learn from our

---

[3] Clifford J. Rodgers, "Clausewitz, Genius and the Rules," *The Journal of Military History* #66 (October 2002): 1167-1176.

experience in Iraq, this paper will focus solely on the universal COIN lessons that can be gleamed from the fight in Afghanistan for two primary reasons. First, stability in Iraq is still tenuous and the great reduction in violence in Iraq along with the official "end of combat operations" makes a case study of this struggle less enlightening in terms of challenges to classical COIN doctrine and strategy. Second, Afghanistan in many ways offers the ultimate challenge in the study of conduct of counterinsurgency because of its geographic isolation and large size, its traditional aversion to any central government, its complex and closed culture, and the ever-present influence of foreign interlopers. This uniquely challenging security environment in Afghanistan will be analyzed in order to prove that despite some success, the nearly decade long war in Afghanistan is not effectively progressing towards meeting the objectives set out in the May 2010 *United States National Security Strategy*, to "disrupt, dismantle and defeat Al-Qaida and its violent extremist affiliates in Afghanistan, Pakistan and around the world."[4]

Likewise, the choice of Somalia as a yardstick to measure the applicability of the recommended changes to FM 3-24 is specifically narrow. The emerging tactics of the Al-Shabaab insurgents in Somalia increasingly mirror those of the Taliban in Afghanistan. These tactics, which include the ruthless enforcement of Sharia law, the forced conscription of local males, the use of low-tech yet spectacular casualty producing weapons have all been copied and transplanted because of their deemed effectiveness for the Taliban. Furthermore, the links that Al-Shabaab has to Muslim extremists, transnational terrorism, and international piracy make this failed-state a significant

---

[4] United States Government, *National Security Strategy* (Washington, DC: Government Printing Office, May 2010), 19.

challenge for Joint Task Force Horn of Africa and for the larger defense establishment of

the United States and its allies.

CHAPTER 2
CLASSICAL COUNTERINSURGENCY DOCTRINE AND THE EVOLUTION OF FM 3-24

When FM 3-24 was published, it had been more than twenty years since the Army or the Marine Corps had updated any doctrine regarding combatting an insurgency. While the guidance it exposes provided a much needed focus to the post-9/11 struggles in Iraq and Afghanistan, it was essentially a starting point or a baseline grounded on the ideas of several well-known population-centric counterinsurgency (COIN) practitioners from conflicts in Algeria and in Malaya in the 1950s and 1960s, in particular, French officer David Galula and British officer Sir Robert Thompson, respectively. Contemporary experts are also consulted but without fail, a population-centric approach is consistently advocated in this new COIN Bible because allegedly campaigns that focus on protecting the population have higher rates of success.[1]

A thorough review of the Army Field Manual (FM) 3-24 / Marine Corps Warfighting Publication (MCWP) 3-33.5, entitled, *Counterinsurgency*, as well as the corresponding Joint Publication of the same title, Joint Publication (JP) 3-24 reveals a set of historically based principles developed to subdue an insurgency. According to many critics, however, there is less practical agreement about these over-generalized principles than classical theorists would have us believe. The reason for defining this manual as classical relates to its heavy reliance on examples provided from the "glorious heyday of revolutionary warfare" between 1950 and 1970 where Thompson and Galula developed

---

[1] John A. Nagl, "Learning and Adapting to Win," *Joint Forces Quarterly*, no. 58 (3rd Quarter 2010): 123.

valuable lessons learned from numerous colonial and Maoists rebellions.[2] It is becoming clearer with each passing month in Afghanistan and Iraq; however, that the examples provided by these recently recognized authors of COIN do not neatly apply to the complexity and scope of the globally linked insurgency we face in these contemporary environments. Hence, the assumptions of classical COIN experts that the population represents the "battleground" and that the "population is a major characteristic of revolutionary war," beg to be re-examined in light of today's religiously-based contemporary and globalized insurgencies.[3]

Counterinsurgency Defined in Doctrine

The basic definitions FM 3-24 uses to frame COIN are valuable points of departure to help frame the remainder of the document. First, FM 3-24 describes that counterinsurgency warfare and its antithesis, insurgency warfare are opposing sides in revolutionary war. It also recognizes that these are two distinctly different types of warfare both residing in a broader category of irregular warfare.[4] Counterinsurgency is defined as "military, paramilitary, political, economic, and civic actions taken by a government to defeat an insurgency," a shared definition with JP 3-24.[5] Conversely, insurgencies "normally seek to achieve one of two goals: to overthrow the existing social order and reallocate power within a single state, or to break away from state control and

---

[2] Frank G. Hoffman, "Neo-Classical Counterinsurgency?," Parameters 37, no. 2 (Summer 2007): 71.

[3] David Galula, *Counterinsurgency Warfare: Theory and Practice* (New York: Praeger Publishers, 1964), 7-8.

[4] US Department of the Army, *Counterinsurgency*, Field Manual 3-24 (Washington DC: GPO, 15 December 2006), 1 1.

[5] Ibid., 1-1.

form an autonomous entity or ungoverned space that they can control."[6] COIN doctrine

also has one primary and enduring theme which is stressed throughout the manual and

suggests that success in COIN depends on learning and adapting faster than the

insurgents. The paradox in this theme; however, is blatantly suggested in the forward of

FM 3-24 which concedes, "You cannot fight former Saddamists and Islamic extremists

the same way you would have fought the Viet Cong, Moros, or Tupamaros." [7] So then,

why is so much of the current doctrine wedded to what more than one critic has decried

as an "outdated and dubious Maoist foundation?"[8]

According to John Nagl (one of the experts assembled by then Lieutenant General

David Petraeus to write the manual at Fort Leavenworth in 2006), "the differences

between previous and current insurgencies are overstated" and that the military who had

largely ignored counterinsurgency warfare over the past three decades, needed to regain a

basic understanding of the fundamental dynamics and challenges posed by an

insurgency.[9] The result in FM 3-24 is that the basic understanding of insurgency and

counterinsurgency is not much different than what existed in Army and Marine Corps

doctrinal publications following the Vietnam era. The new manual is applied largely

within the narrow context of the American counterinsurgencies in Afghanistan and Iraq.

It was intended to be of immediate use to forces already engaged in combat or those

preparing to deploy.

---

[6] Army Field Manual 3-24, 1-2.

[7] Ibid., Preface.

[8] Ralph Peters, "Progress and Peril: New Counterinsurgency Manual Cheats on the History Exam," *Armed Forces Journal International*, no. 144, (February 2007): 34.

[9] John A. Nagl, Constructing the Legacy of Field Manual 3-24, *Joint Forces Quarterly*, no. 58 (3rd Quarter, 2010): 118.

FM 3-24 provides a menu of eight principles, five contemporary imperatives, ten paradoxes, and host of proposed best practices. For example, the basic American approach to COIN forged over the course of the Cold War focused on a double pronged attack designed to defeat the insurgents with military force while also intervening to alter the grievances that led to the insurgency and the reasons to fight. Furthermore, it is difficult to argue certain basic principles presented in current COIN doctrine such as unity of effort, understanding the environment (society and culture), intelligence as a driver for operations, and providing security for the population under the rule of law, because they have been validated repeatedly over the last century of warfare. COIN imperatives such as managing information, learning and adapting, and empowering lower-level leaders also already have a place in American conventional leadership training. It is the introduction of so-called "paradoxes" of COIN; however, that make FM 3-24 unique from earlier counterinsurgency publications. Two of these paradoxes include: "the more force you use, the less effective you are," and that "tactical success guarantees nothing" reflect the idea that at its core, counterinsurgency is focused on winning the hearts and minds of the population.[10]

Recent criticism of FM 3-24 has been somewhat muted due to the reduction of violence in Iraq. The reasons for the apparent progress in Iraq; however, is the result of many variables including the negotiated deals with insurgent factions through "Awakening Councils" or "Concerned Local Citizen" (CLC) groups and not primarily due to the implementation of this new COIN doctrine.[11] Furthermore, most military and

---

[10] Army Field Manual 3-24, 1-27, 1-28.

[11] Stephen Biddle, "The New US Army/Marine Corps Counterinsurgency Field Manual as Political Science and Political Praxis," *Review Symposium* 6, no. 2 (June 2008): 349.

foreign policy experts remain hesitant to prognosticate on the future stability of Iraq as American forces depart and remain only in smaller numbers as advisors and trainers. The other problem with much of the criticism of FM 3-24 is that much of it fails to offer alternative courses of action to the population-centric framework offered by the COIN manual's team of writers.

Classic Counterinsurgency Critiques

The most telling criticisms of FM 3-24 fall into three general categories. First, there has been a recent call by some military leaders and defense experts such as Colonel Gian Gentile, a history professor at the United States Military Academy, who effectively argue that we need to start over and revise COIN doctrine in the same manner that the U.S. Army did when it reconstructed Active Defense Doctrine between 1976 and 1982 to produce the arguably more effective doctrine of Airland Battle. The second and much more widely critiqued flaw of the current COIN manual relates to its over-reliance on population-centric theories developed from classic COIN experts such as David Galula and Sir Robert Thompson combating Maoist insurgents and fighting anticolonial conflicts early in the Cold War. Finally, there are several noted COIN experts including David Kilcullen and Steven Metz who suggest that U.S. defense leaders need to fundamentally rethink COIN strategy and doctrine with a focus on combating a global insurgency, rather than one that is focused on a single nation-state.

The proposal to "deconstruct" the current doctrine exposed in FM 3-24 may seem draconian, but it is not without merit. Colonel Gentile's argument to start over and remake our COIN doctrine is based on two valid objections. He concludes that many Army and Marine Corps leaders were engaged in the fight in either Afghanistan or Iraq when the draft FM 3-24 was sent out to the field for review and so, it did not undergo the type of rigorous debate that such a foundational document to our current and future way of war should have received.[12] There was simply not enough time to gather and incorporate existing lessons learned and alternative viewpoints before it was published.

Gentile's second complaint is that military leaders and defense experts have been influenced by analysts such as Tom Ricks and John Nagl into accepting COIN lessons of Galula and Thompson as proven techniques when the facts do not support such blind obedience especially considering that the global security environment we face now is so radically different than anything seen in fighting colonial insurgencies in Algeria and Indochina. One of the examples Gentile uses relates to the war in Vietnam. Advocates of classic COIN theory claim that one of the successes that did arise out of the U.S. experience in Vietnam was the pacification program employed by General Creighton Abrams. While for a short time the program did secure the countryside in South Vietnam, the cause of this limited success was less the effective separation of the insurgents from the population as proposed by classic theorists, but rather the deliberate destruction of vast portions of the countryside by American firepower that essentially forced the depopulation of those areas.[13]

Finally, Gentile makes the argument that because of these significant flaws, FM 3-24, like the Active Defense Doctrine before it in 1976, is insufficient to guide our soldiers in battle. He suggests that defense leaders must now take the time to reconstruct our COIN doctrine to make up for these deficiencies in a similar way that "Airland Battle

---

[12] Gian P. Gentile, "Time for the Deconstruction of Field Manual 3-24," *Joint Forces Quarterly*, no. 58 (3rd Quarter, 2010): 116.

[13] Gian P. Gentile, "Freeing the Army from the Counterinsurgency Straitjacket," *Joint Forces Quarterly*, no. 58 (3rd Quarter, 2010): 122.

rose from the ashes of Active Defense Doctrine after four years of deliberate, open debate." [14] This idea has merit, but one must also consider that the U.S. and its coalition partners remain embroiled in two counterinsurgencies that continue to sap our resources and kill our soldiers. If a renewed effort to deconstruct and then reconstruct the COIN doctrine is entertained by the defense establishment, the aforementioned costs must also be considered and therefore, the premise that we can afford four years to complete such a review is also not realistic. While a critical debate is required, this process must be timely and not significantly add to the protracted nature of the ongoing conflicts in Afghanistan and Iraq. However, to ignore the need for this review process may not only further protract these conflicts; it may result in a strategic loss that will almost surely have negative ramifications to U.S. national security.

The most common critique of the current COIN manual is that it is willfully based on the lessons of classic COIN practitioners including David Galula and Sir David Thompson whose experiences in Algeria and Indochina were detailed in *Counterinsurgency Warfare: Theory and Practice (1964)* and *Defeating Communist Insurgency* (1966), respectively. These anti-colonial insurgent struggles were just like all other counterinsurgencies - unique. Further, after thorough historical review, they were not as successful as originally advertised. While each of these counterinsurgency examples provide valuable learning points for what can be effective when engaging in specific types of insurgencies, the tendency to seek new ideas from these old conflicts leads the U.S. to errantly fight the last war. [15] Those who rigidly follow these classicists

---

[14] "Time for the Deconstruction of Field Manual 3-24," 117.

[15] Steven Metz, *Rethinking Insurgency* (Carlisle, PA: Strategic Studies Institute, June 2007) http://www.StrategicStudiesInstitute.army.mil/pubs/display.cfm?pubID=790 (assessed on October 4, 2010): 3.

myopically ignore the uniqueness of these two colonial examples and over-simplify the relevant principles that can be drawn from them. Accordingly, Frank G. Hoffman contends that there is not as much common ground between the masters of counterinsurgency as the classicists argue and perhaps more importantly, the factors which motivate contemporary insurgencies are "not reflected by broad historical trends, nor do they follow previously recognized phases."[16]

Also significant to this critique is the idea proposed by Dr. Paul Melshen that developing a COIN strategy based primarily on these classicists is a "simplistic" analysis that would offer "prescriptions" which would not effectively account for the complexities we face in contemporary counterinsurgent conflicts. He does not argue that the study of and evaluation of past insurgent conflicts is not valuable in the development of COIN doctrine; however, he advises that it must also include experience from recent personal involvement in COIN. Melshen suggests this personal involvement will provide an understanding of the "unique parameters of the conflict – military, political, sociological, religious, cultural, ethnic, tribal, economic and a multiplicity of others."[17]

The third general category of valid criticism that targets FM 3-24 focuses on those who believe that the U.S. defense establishment needs to rethink its doctrinal approach to COIN by recognizing that the current wars in Afghanistan and Iraq are better understood as campaigns in a larger global insurgency. Even David Kilcullen, who had previously been a contributor to FM 3-24 and classical COIN theory, now recognizes that a "traditional counterinsurgency paradigm will not work for the present war: instead, a

---

[16] Frank G. Hoffman, "Neo-Classical Counterinsurgency?," 73.

[17] Paul Melshen, "Mapping Out a Counterinsurgency Campaign Plan: Critical Considerations in Counterinsurgency Campaigning," *Small Wars and Insurgencies* 18, no. 4 (December, 2007): 667.

fundamental reappraisal is needed, to develop methods effective against a globalized insurgency."[18] Steven Metz from the Army War College also concludes that the reason why the U.S. and other liberal democracies must rethink the strategic context of COIN is because contemporary insurgency is often associated with the tactic of transnational terrorism. He further challenges classical COIN theory stating that contemporary insurgency cannot be conceptualized as "a variant of traditional, Clausewitzian war" and that "Clausewitz may have been right that war is always fought for political purposes, but not all armed conflict is war."[19] Perhaps even more damning to FM 3-24 is the idea that "resolving an insurgency requires extensive social reengineering" and that "distinct types of counterinsurgencies require entirely different U.S. responses" in order to avoid the lethal and costly effects of protracted conflict.[20]

Two recent examples of counterinsurgency operations that challenge the current strategic approach taken by the United States include: the recent defeat of the Tamil Tiger separatists by Sri Lankan government forces in that protracted and bloody insurgency, and the latest critique that flawed U.S. assumptions will thwart success against the Taliban and Al Qaeda in Afghanistan. First, in Sri Lanka, it was the institution of harsh principles by government forces that stand in direct contrast to the population-centric teachings of classical COIN that contributed to ending this violent insurgency last May which had raged since 1983. Principles such as: "ignoring domestic and international criticism, objecting to all negotiations, regulating the media, denying

---

[18] David Kilcullen, "Countering Global Insurgency," *The Journal of Strategic Studies* 28, no. 4 (August 2005): 614.

[19] Metz, *Rethinking Insurgency* , 49.

[20] Ibid., 52.

ceasefires, and allowing military commanders complete operational freedom" are included in this so-called "Rajapaksa Model" of successful Sri Lankan COIN.[21]

The Sri Lankan COIN model is exceptional and it helps prove that every insurgency requires a unique approach rather than a scientific classical approach. A complementary critique has been leveled on the Obama Administration claiming it has relied on false assumptions and a rigid adherence to classic COIN theory in fighting the counterinsurgency in Afghanistan. For example, in terms of a regional campaign within the context of a larger global insurgency, the U.S has made the incorrect assumptions (based on the extensive resources that continue to be expended) that: "Afghanistan is of far greater importance to Al Qaeda than any other geographic location," and that "the U.S. has sufficient popular support and resources" to successfully defeat this insurgency before those resources are exhausted.[22] Unfortunately, the facts do not support this strategic mindset and call into question whether a counterinsurgency operation is the best method to achieve the intended national objectives outlined in the 2010 *National Security Strategy*. A successful COIN outcome will likely have little effect on the threat imposed by Al Qaeda even if the Taliban is completely destroyed.

There has also been a growing argument that COIN as defined by FM 3-24 is not even the appropriate strategy for achieving ISAF's objectives in Afghanistan. Some defense experts suggest the nature of this conflict is more accurately characterized as a fight for stability with various armed criminal groups rather than a strong core of Taliban insurgents whose primary objectives are to defeat the Coalition and the central

---

[21] Neil Smith, "Understanding Sri Lanka's Defeat of the Tamil Tigers," *Joint Forces Quarterly*, no. 59 (4th Quarter 2010): 40.

[22] Mark Schrecker, "US Strategy in Afghanistan: Flawed Assumptions Will Lead to Ultimate Failure," *Joint Forces Quarterly*, no. 59 (4th Quarter 2010): 76.

government in order to expel foreigners, consolidate power and extort wealth. The theme of this argument is that the Taliban have been marginalized and weakened by criminality to the point that they are no longer relevant. This is not to say that Afghanistan should be left to its own vices; however, the idea that ISAF's efforts there should be more narrowly focused on combating the hierarchies of the many organized criminal elements is worthy of consideration. Deep fissures within the Taliban have been verified through secondary data reports and interviews with current and former Taliban leaders and signal the breakdown of the Taliban from a unifying insurgent force into a loosely organized criminal element.[23] Therefore, the idea that the massive resources ISAF is currently expending through the vigorous execution of COIN should be narrowed to focus on the criminal elements in this perpetually violent so-called "Chaotic Cannabalistic State" warrants consideration if the insurgency has indeed morphed.[24]

In summary, the tenets of classic COIN theory which establish the foundation of FM 3-24 continue to generate critical review by a growing tide of detractors who argue that the entire document needs to be completely deconstructed; that it is tied too closely to population-centric approaches based on isolated colonial insurgencies of the 1950s and 1960s; and that the current COIN strategy does not account for the myriad of factors that comprise this global and transnational nature of the insurgency we face from Al Qaeda. While each of these general critiques has merit, the cynics also recognize the fact that some classic COIN principles maintain relevance. The overriding theme is no two insurgencies are exactly alike and any attempt to apply a scientific formula to mirror

---

[23] Kevin Meredith, Sergio Villarreal, and Mitchel Wilkinson, "Afghanistan: The De-evolution of Insurgency," *Small Wars Journal* (October 7, 2010): 10.

[24] Ibid., 21.

success (i.e. Henri Jomini) in COIN will be futile. While the American military may not have the luxury of several years to analyze, debate and rewrite FM 3-24, it can and should revise the current doctrine to reflect the complex nature and global reach of the modern insurgency. Insurgency or insurgency-like conflicts are expected to dominate the next several decades of warfare given the increasingly multi-polar balance of power in the world. Therefore, it is imperative that military and civilian leaders are well versed in the application of effective counterinsurgency techniques and principles in order to develop the appropriate campaign design necessary to meet national security objectives. The following case study on the Afghanistan counterinsurgency will facilitate several recommendations for specific revisions to FM 3-24.

CHAPTER 3
AFGHANISTAN CASE STUDY

To understand the unique security environment that the United States and its coalition allies within the International Security Forces – Afghanistan (ISAF) face, it is necessary to examine the important characteristics which make this historically war torn environment one of the most difficult places in the world to fight and win in any form of warfare and particularly precarious for counterinsurgency (COIN) operations. The three general characteristics which have most influenced the ability of the International Assistance Forces Afghanistan (ISAF) to execute a COIN strategy include the country's historical background, the complex tribal culture that has historically resisted foreign interference and central government control, and the influence of external actors who actively interfere. In order for Western military and civilian leaders to operate effectively in this complex security environment, significant preparation is required. This preparation must result in the advanced understanding of Afghan culture that goes beyond simple cultural awareness and grows into cultural appreciation.

Historical Background

Historically, several patterns have emerged over the last two centuries that help to define Afghanistan today. First, because of its strategically important location that links Central, West and South Asia, the control of Afghanistan has been continuously contested and this has resulted in some benefits for the Afghans, but more often it has led to unprecedented suffering during conflicts between great external powers (see Appendix A). The second trend, which explains a lot about the protracted nature of the current fight there, is the traditional lack of an effective government. Only in the face of foreign invaders have fiercely independent tribes been able to set aside their differences against a common foe. In fact, the majority Pashtun tribe has never been fully subjugated by a foreign invader. The final historical trend, which is also significant in the current struggle in Afghanistan, is the pervasive role of Islam. Despite several foreign attempts to destroy and marginalize Islam (specifically Genghis Khan and the Soviets), Islam remains a part of the fabric of Afghanistan and there has been no separation of religion and politics. In fact, Muslim religious leaders in Afghanistan commonly also serve a role politically.[1]

Afghan Tribal Culture

Culture is significant to understanding Afghanistan because when combined with the unforgiving terrain and the nation's tragic history, cultural factors will have a dominant role in determining the success of this most recent employment of the new COIN doctrine. Culture has been defined as a "dynamic social system," containing the values, beliefs, behaviors, and norms of a "specific group, organization, society or other collectivity" learned, shared, internalized, and changeable by all members of the society.[2] A deeper review of culture suggests that cultural considerations should ideally be reviewed at each of the levels of war (tactical, operational, and strategic) and that leaders, strategists and policymakers need to account for their own "cultural lens" before they act or engage with another culture. Colonel Jiyul Kim suggests that an Analytic Cultural Framework for Strategy and Policy (ACFSP) based on the fundamental cultural

---

[1] *Afghan History*, in Afghanan Dot Net, http://www.afghanan.net/afghanistan/history.htm (accessed on 26 October, 2010).

[2] Jeff Watson, "Language and Culture Training: Separate Paths?," *Military Review* 90, no. 2 (March-April, 2008): 93.

dimensions of identity (the basis for defining identity and its linkage to interests), political culture (the structure of power and decision making), and resilience (the capacity or ability to resist, adapt or succumb to external forces) can assist in determining both action and behavior.[3] Regardless of how culture is analyzed, there has been a growing recognition by the U.S. defense establishment since the end of the Cold War and more recently because of experiences in Iraq and Afghanistan that cultural appreciation is vital to success at the tactical and operational level. For the U.S. military and government officials deployed abroad, the initial efforts at understanding culture focused on perfunctory cultural awareness classes that proved inadequate. Since then, a cultural awakening has evolved due to the protracted nature of COIN operations and because of the innovation and dedication of leaders across the whole of government.

In Afghanistan, cultural understanding is a formidable task for several reasons. The first significant hurdle in cultural understanding involves the two main Afghan languages Dari and Pashto. Written and verbal communications are critical representations of every culture; however, Dari and Pashto complicate the understanding of Afghan culture by Westerners because both languages were adapted from the Arabic alphabet, but neither is related to Arabic and each includes additional letters not found in Arabic. Furthermore, these alphabets do not include any symbols which represent vowels and this makes a letter-by-letter translation from Dari or Pashto into English impossible.[4] Hence, there are significant barriers to effective and accurate communication throughout Afghanistan, even with the best translator or interpreter.

---

[3] Jiyul Kim, "Cultural Dimensions of Strategy and Policy," Letort Paper (Carlisle, PA: Strategic Studies Institute, 2008): 10.

[4] Ingrid Rader, "Shaping the Information Environment in Afghanistan," *Small Wars Journal*, July 2010, http://smallwarsjournal.com (accessed on August 15, 2010).

Another daunting challenge to understanding Afghan culture is related to its sheer complexity: the Afghan population is extremely diverse both ethnically and demographically. The country has been historically divided into numerous sections and regions that have been supplementary grouped by tribe, gender, age, education, occupation and locale (urban or agrarian). Ethnically, Pashtuns are the largest majority and make up forty-two percent of the population. Conversely, the combination of the other major ethnicities such as the Tajiks, the Uzbeks and the Hazarans outnumber the Pashtuns.[5] The Pashtuns, however, make up the majority of the insurgent population and they have also been the dominant political force in the last century. Understanding the Pashtuns and their tribal social code called the *Pashtunwali* is therefore critical to Afghan cultural appreciation. Sun Tzu professed that if you "know your enemies and know yourself, you will not be imperiled in a hundred battles; if you do not know your enemies but do know yourself, you will win one and lose one; if you do not know your enemies nor yourself, you will be imperiled in every single battle."[6] To know the Pashtun Taliban insurgent, it is necessary to comprehend the *Pashtunwali*. This code defines the roles and responsibilities in the family unit, the role of the tribe in daily life, and the overarching role of religion for the Pashtuns.

The Pashtunwali Code

The *Pashtunwali* or "way of the Pashtuns" is a social code that is the "unwritten, democratic, socio-political culture, law and ideology of the Pashtun society inherited from their forefathers and carried on to the present generation and remains a dominant

---

[5] The Central Intelligence Agency, *The World Factbook*, https://www.cia.gov/library/publications/the-world-factbook/gcos/af.html (accessed on November 1, 2010).

[6] Samuel B. Griffith, *Sun Tzu: The Art of War*, (New York: Oxford University Press, 1962), 50.

force of Pashtun culture and identity."[7] Understanding the code is extremely helpful in describing the actions and behaviors of Pashtuns. While this code is centuries old, it is still relatively young in its influence on Pashtun cultural and socio-economic structure. The best example that highlights the *Pashtunwali* is the offer of safe haven to Osama Bin Laden after the attacks on September, 11th 2001. The United States gave the Taliban government an ultimatum: turn over the 9/11 mastermind to U.S. custody or face destruction. The Taliban Government comprised mainly of Pashtuns, would not in any way comply with U.S. demands. Their failure to comply did not have anything to do with logic or the ultimatum; it had everything to do with culture. Bin Laden was their guest and guests are protected even at the cost of the protector's life according to the *Pashtunwali*. This particular tenet of the code is called, *melmastia* and it means hospitality. The personal honor of a Pashtun male is directly related to his ability to provide appropriate hospitality and protection for any guest who asks for assistance. Even if the guest is an enemy, he will still be offered *melmastia*. The Pashtun government of the Taliban provided *melmastia* to Bin Laden and it was the collective honor of the nation that was challenged by U.S. demands to hand him over. A complete listing of the major tenets of the *Pashtunwali* can be further reviewed in Appendix B.

The most critical tenant of the *Pashtunwali* is *nang* which translates to honor. For Pashtuns defending one's honor is paramount among all other social frameworks and typically involves a display of personal independence including the ability to exact justice

---

[7] Ali Nawaz Memon, "*Pashtunwali* Code of conduct for Pashtuns," Sindh Development Institute, entry posted February 13, 2008, http://sindhdi.wordpress.com/2008/02/13/*Pashtunwali*-code-of-conduct-of-pashtuns/ (accessed November 2, 2010).

and to protect women, children, property, and guests.[8] The male-dominated Afghan culture is infused with this concept of honor and of settling differences in an honorable fashion man-to-man and face-to-face. The initial responses of most Afghans to the U.S. cruise missile attacks aimed at Al Qaeda training sites in Khowst Province was one of outrage because "Washington had not challenged Mr. Bin Laden to a fair fight, and attacked without warning."[9] The realities of modern warfare since the Soviet invasion have changed some of the ways Pashtuns apply *nang* to their tactics; nevertheless, it remains a powerful force that dominates Pashtun culture.

Closely tied to personal honor is *badal* or revenge. The reason this principle is significant to COIN is because it highlights the previously cited paradox from U.S. Army Field Manual 3-24, "the more force you use, the less effective you are."[10] Killing insurgent Taliban fighters simply means you have produced more insurgents as relatives of those killed are now committed to avenging that death regardless of whether or not it was justified. Ritual killings to avenge an insult or a death have been commonplace in Pashtun society for centuries. Honor must be maintained and this is most often satisfied through revenge. Undoubtedly many of those identified as insurgents by coalition forces in Afghanistan have no prevailing political or religious motivation for their participation in violence. They are more likely involved in a blood feud designed to regain lost honor.

---

[8] *Pashtunwali*" in Afghan Roma Web Portal, https://ronna-afghan.harmonieweb.org/Pages/*Pashtunwali*.aspx, (accessed 5 November, 2010).

[9] Anonymous, *Through our Enemies' Eyes: Osama bin Laden*, Radical Islam, and the Future of America (Washington, DC: Brassey's Inc, 2002), 155.

[10] Army Field Manual 3-24, 1-27.

The Role of the Tribe

Special Forces Major Jim Gant describes Afghan tribes as "the most important military, political and cultural unit in the country" and that for our COIN strategy to work against the Taliban, coalition efforts need to work "first and forever" with the tribes.[11] After the family, the next most significant identity that most Afghans submit to, regardless of ethnic origin, is the tribe. The tribe is the basic building block in the social fabric of this population and for Pashtuns, it is governed by the *Pashtunwali*. It is through tribal organized councils, called *jirgas* and *shuras*, that tribal members meet to dispense justice and provide a means of conflict resolution within the tribe as well as resolve disputes between tribes. For the Afghans, tribes embody the ideals about how a society should be organized and they stress values such as egalitarianism, mutual caring, sharing, reciprocity, collective responsibility, group solidarity, family, community, civility, and even democracy.[12]

One of the other important connections between the *Pashtunwali* and the tribe involves the aforementioned tenet of *nang* or honor. Honor is as important to the tribe as it is to the individual. The restoration of lost honor is often both an individual and collective responsibility shared by the entire tribe. This is significant to understand because most Afghan tribes considers themselves Pashtuns first and Muslims second. Along those same lines, there are some vulnerable fault lines between sharia law and the *Pashtunwali* which can be exploited to isolate radical Islamists within the insurgency.

---

[11] Jim Gant, "One Tribe at a Time: A Strategy for Success in Afghanistan," Steven Pressfield Online, the Warrior Ethos, entry posted September 29, 2009, http://blog.stevenpressfield.com, (accessed on November 12, 2010).

[12] David Ronfeldt, *In Search of How Societies Work: Tribes the First and Forever Form, Rand* (Santa Monica, CA: Rand Corporation, (December 2006): 59.

Those like Gant who advocate a culturally focused approach to counterinsurgency believe that the best strategy to deal with Taliban insurgency is a renewed effort to engage the tribes with Tactical Engagement Teams (TETs) in order to use the traditional tribal authorities to help with community security and assistance and drive out the Taliban.[13] Others, like Khalil Nouri and Terry Green believe that a new strategic partner who is a business czar versed in tribal affairs (analogous to former King Zahir Shah) is required to steer the tribes out of this conflict. They further stipulate that this business czar "should not only be familiar with the current vital requirement on the ground, but also have deep tribal perception, affiliation and flamboyancy to restore the regional tribal balances and convey prosperity."[14] While both of these innovative solutions have merit, current U.S. COIN doctrine aggregates these tribes into the people which assumes a consistency and homogeneity that does not exist in Afghanistan. The cultural lens which is so important in understanding a religious or ethnically based insurgency does not exist in current doctrine. Hence, a counterinsurgency campaign focused on winning tribes instead of the people has yet to be seriously considered.

Another worthy consideration that highlights the importance of Afghan tribes involves the theory of organizational structure and how it may affect the outcome of the current conflict. Applied to military organizations, this theory describes how the distribution of power internal to an organization in armed conflict inspires its members to

---

[13] Gant, "One Tribe at a Time: A Strategy for Success in Afghanistan."

[14] Khalil Nouri and Terry Green, "Afghanistan Needs a Tribal Business Czar to Work with the US," http://www.usborderfirereport.com/afghanistan_needs_a_tribal_busin.htm, (accessed on November 13, 2010).

outlast rivals.[15] The Pashtun tribe, which serves as the organization structure for the

Taliban insurgency, has a centralized structure under Mullah Omar despite increasing

internal fracturing. The other major armed group participating in the fighting, Hizb-i-

Islami, led by Hekmatyar, also exhibits a centralized structure. Whether by chance or

design, the structure of these fighting organizations in Afghanistan may directly affect

their success in the same way that the organization of the Karzai government and its

coalition partners will determine their success. Likewise, the ability of one or the other

of the antagonists to effect the organization of their foe, will improve the likelihood of

their own victory. In general, centralized organizations are most effective, especially

those with a safe haven to protect it from interference.[16] Therefore, the tribes which

dominate the Afghan insurgency are currently well situated organizationally to outlast the

current government and its ISAF partners unless their safe havens in Pakistan can be

denied or a change in their organizational structure can be exacted by exploiting the

fragmented opposition and regional rivalries within the tribal leadership leading to more

decentralization. For a more detailed overview of this model proposed by Abdulkader

Sinno, see Appendix C.

The Afghan Family

The lowest level of social organization in Afghan society is the family. Again, the

Pashtunwali code plays a central role in guiding behavior within the family; however,

there is a level of complexity and privacy within Afghan families that must be understood

and respected by those engaged in COIN. The Afghan family is "endogamous (with

---

[15] Abdulkader H. Sinno, *Organizations at War in Afghanistan and Beyond* (Ithaca: Cornell University Press, 2008): 11.

[16] Ibid., Pg 17.

26

parallel and cross-cousin marriages preferred), patriarchal (authority vested in male elders), patrilineal (inheritance through the male line), and patrilocal (girl moves to husband's place of residence on marriage)."[17] While polygymy (multiple wives) is still officially permitted, it is increasingly less common due to the costs incurred. Through the last three decades of conflict in Afghanistan, family solidarity has become even more significant through extended kinship. War, governmental corruption, and poverty have forced this extended family to become the primary social and economic enabler in the absence of government. These extended families are often characterized by three to four generations living in one compound or spread out in a single valley.[18] From birth through death, an Afghan's individual, social, economic, political rights, and obligations are determined within the family. In return, the family provides their security. Tensions often exist in these extended families as there is sometimes violent competition for power, authority and inheritance.

The core of the Afghan family rests with the senior woman reigning at the top of the power hierarchy within the household. "Afghan society regards women as the perpetuators of the ideals of the society" and as such "they symbolize honor -- of family, community and nation -- and must be controlled as well as protected so as to maintain moral purity."[19] However, male authority within the family is paramount and age is universally respected. Male prestige and family honor are both tied to the accepted right

[17] Peter R. Blood, ed. *Afghanistan: A Country Study* (Washington: GPO for the Library of Congress, 2001) http://countriestudies.us/afghanistan/57.htm (accessed 14 October, 2010).

[18] Ibid.

[19] Butler, Rhett A., "Afghan Gender Roles," http://www.mongabay.com/history/afghanistan/afghanistan-gender_roles.html (accessed on November 12, 2010).

that males can control female behavior. Independent female action is therefore regarded as a shameful loss of male control and is condemned socially, bringing humiliation to the entire family. Even among the urban elite in Kabul, social pressures force women to be dependent on men. Domestic abuse against women remains a significant problem for Afghan women despite a newly drafted law by the Afghan Parliament that is intended to eliminate and reject these old cultural practices that have led to an estimated 2,300 attempted suicides by females each year.[20]

Nevertheless, women are able to maintain leverage in several important ways that are often overlooked. First, older women in the family are typically designated to manage the families' food supplies after the harvest to ensure that it is distributed effectively over the year until the next harvest. This is an important responsibility because if the grain is not apportioned correctly, the family must go into debt or starve. Another point of leverage for females in this male dominated social environment is through the use of subtle non-conformity which can greatly affect the reputation and honor of the family in the tribe. For instance, within the *Pahstunwali* tenet of *melmestia* or hospitality; a woman who does not display the requisite courtesy to an invited guest may purposely bring shame on the entire extended family. The influence of women within the Afghan family remains substantial even if not by Western standards and a thorough understanding of the role of women can assist those fighting a war of ideas with the Taliban by offering other avenues to improve intelligence gathering and to exploit information operations through effective messaging. This can be particularly effective if trained counterinsurgent women are employed to socially engage Afghan women.

---

[20] Lynsey Addario, "Veiled Rebellion," *National Geographic* 218, no. 6 (December 2010): 53.

Religion

Within the tribal and ethnic diversity in Afghanistan, religion serves as a unifying factor that greatly influences the daily lives of Afghans and also serves as the primary tool for the insurgent Taliban to solicit support from the population. Islam is the central, pervasive influence throughout Afghan society; religious observances punctuate the rhythm of each day and season. Additionally, every year, thousands of Afghans participate in the Hajj, traveling to Mecca in Saudi Arabia. More than ninety-nine percent of Afghans consider themselves Muslims and more than eighty percent practice Sunni Islam and belong to the Hanafi Islamic school. The other ten to nineteen percent practice Shi'a Islam and the majority of those follow the Twelver branch with smaller numbers of Ismailis.[21] Until the rise of the Taliban (which means religious student) in the fall of 1994, Islam in Afghanistan was egalitarian and characterized by honesty, frugality, generosity, virtuousness, piousness, fairness, truthfulness, tolerance and respect for others. Since the rise of the Taliban, *Sharia* law has been imposed in several Afghan provinces that lack central government control.

Just as a hierarchy exists in Afghan families, there is also a religious hierarchy in Afghanistan which consists of several levels. While any Muslim male may lead prayer, the *mullah* is the religious official who officiates at a local mosque and is responsible to ensure their communities are versed in Islamic rituals and behaviors. *Mullahs* are primarily part-time religious teachers in rural areas, while in more urban areas; they often serve the population full-time. They are chosen and supported by the communities they serve and although they receive minimal support from the Islamic Republic of

---

[21] *The World Factbook.*

Afghanistan, the majority of their shelter and support comes directly from the community they serve. Significantly, *mullahs* also arbitrate religious disputes and officiate at major life events including births, deaths and marriages. Because religious disputes sometimes have political overtones and because *mullahs* rarely share consenting opinions, they can often unintentionally cause disruption and dissent among their community of followers.[22] Regardless, it is important to identify who these religious leaders are because they do have an influence on the behavior of their followers and are often the keys to resolving disputes, especially when the tribal leader and the *mullah* are the same individual.

A natural tension exists between Islam and the *Pashtunwali* within the population. The practice of extremely restrictive *Sharia* law directly conflicts with the *Pashtunwali* which promotes tolerance, dignity and individual choice. In an effort to prove their superior piety, the Taliban enforce a strict interpretation of *Sharia* law which reflects a view that is more likely meant to satisfy foreign influences rather than to comply with Afghan cultural norms. Furthermore, it shows that the Taliban continue to display complete disregard for the inherent complexities involved with this type of religious law and the checks and balances that must be applied across the whole society.

Because the current Afghan government has been incapable of exercising the rule of law, many Afghans turn to the Taliban to provide some level of structure and accountability to their lives, even if it means *Sharia* law and shadow governments run by the Taliban. Also, by making the insurgency about religion, the Taliban not only gains additional recruits, it also protracts and widens the conflict because "religious-based

---

[22] "Islam in Afghanistan," http://english.turkcebilgi.com/Islam+in+Afghanistan (accessed November 12, 2010).

conflicts tend to make it more difficult to attain political compromise or settlement."[23]   A

cursory review of warfare in the last half century proves that religious wars are often

much more destructive and cause higher casualties than other wars fought primarily over

ethnicity or ideology.

By widening the conflict to be perceived as a religious war, both the Taliban and

Al Qaeda incite fellow Muslims to join this violent jihad as a test of their religious faith.

With religion as the focus of the conflict, the domestic and international order is

threatened in a way that closely mirrors events in the seventeenth century. When religion

interferes with the state's ability to negotiate, the killing will likely continue even after

there is any political, social or economic utility in continuing the fight. Also, religiously

incited violence tends to embolden religious authority often resulting in authoritarian

regimes that are less stable. Recent events in Egypt, Tunisia, Yemen and Libya illustrate

the fragility of authoritarian regimes whether or not they are religiously inspired.

Religious authoritarian regimes are particularly dangerous both internally and

externally. Internally, these regimes are fragile because any challenge or critique of a

government policy becomes indistinguishable from a challenge to God and hence there is

no mechanism for dissent. As a point of reference, in the forty-two religious civil wars

from 1942 to 2000, thirty-four involved governments and rebels who were considered

Islamic; far more than any other religion. Externally, these regimes also exhibit more

aggressive behavior towards neighboring states and therefore suggest a more violent

---

[23] Frank G. Hoffman, "Neo-Classical Counterinsurgency?," *Parameters* 37, no.2 (Summer 2007): 78.

world environment.[24] An historical example of religious conflict in the seventeenth century that reveals a similar trend for Christianity occurred during the Reformation.

The Ideology of the Taliban Insurgent

In casual conversation with ordinary Afghan villagers, interlopers quickly realize that while most of the population recognizes that the Taliban do not follow the tenets of Islam or even those of the *Pastunwali*, many still support their cause (even if tacitly). What about the ideology of the Taliban appeals to Afghans even though many of their terrorist tactics including suicide bombings kill far more fellow Afghans than Coalition soldiers? The reasons are complex and call into question some of the basic strategies of COIN doctrine.

Mullah Omar is the spiritual leader and founder of the Afghan Taliban. He remains the leader of the organization while leading from the Quetta *Shura* from Pakistan. Although he recently released a statement trying to separate the nationalist Taliban ideology from that of Al Qaeda, the U.S. has not recognized any change in the partnership with Al Qaeda which led to the American invasion in 2001. In fact, the U.S. has stipulated that Mullah Omar and his fundamentalist organization remain aligned with Al Qaeda and are not reconcilable.[25] While there are many other insurgent groups and other major leaders in the insurgency including Gulbiddin Hekmatyar, Jalauddin and Siraj Haqqani, and Baitullah and Haqimullah Mehsud who may be willing to reconcile, most of these groups appear to be united in the ideology that the foreign forces need to be

---

[24] Monica Duffy Toft, "Getting Religion," *International Security*, 31, no. 4, (Spring 2007): 97-131.

[25] *Frontline*, "Behind Taliban Lines," Public Broadcasting Service, http://www.pbs.org/wgbh/pages/frontline/talibanlines/map/ (accessed November 12, 2010).

expelled from Afghanistan.[26] The other major points of ideology that these groups seem to share with Al Qaeda include the replacement of democratic values with Islamic values and the idea of a modern Islamic Caliphate. Beyond these shared values, each of the more than 150 insurgent groups has their own specific goals and objectives. Hence, many strategic experts have concluded that this loose affiliation amounts to little more than a vision statement rather than a detailed end-ways-means strategy for the future. In fact, no insurgent group affiliated with the Taliban has offered any specifics on the future of Afghanistan other than expelling foreign forces and imposing Islamic values through *Sharia* law.

Still other defense experts such as David Kilcullen and Steven Metz suggest that the conflict in Afghanistan is simply one theater in a global jihad. There is evidence that "Islamist groups within theaters follow general ideological or strategic approaches aligned with Al Qaeda pronouncements and share a common tactical style and operational lexicon."[27] Not surprisingly, many leaders in the global jihad are related by birth or by marriage. For instance, Osama Bin Laden's marriage to Mullah Omar's daughter ensured that his base of operations in Afghanistan would be protected. Metz asserts that the risk of internal conflicts like the one in Afghanistan is not simply that the global insurgency will win in that nation-state but more importantly, it will generate other adverse effects including "the destabilization of regions, resource flows and markets; the

---

[26] Ibid.

[27] David Kilcullen, "Countering Global Insurgency," *The Journal of Strategic Studies 28, no. 4* (August 2005): 598.

blossoming of international crime; humanitarian disasters; transnational terrorism; and so forth."[28]

It is also worth considering that the insurgency in Afghanistan is not an insurgency at all, but rather a coalesced group of criminal elements that have organized to fight the government and the coalition because they are a threat to their drug trafficking. The ideology of the criminal organization is much simpler: money, power and prestige for the group. The idea is that Afghanistan has become a "Chaotic Cannibalistic State" in perpetual conflict with separate criminal elements feeding on each other internally until the host (a foreign force) is introduced causing a feeding frenzy on the host until the injured host must withdraw.[29]   This is significant because if it is true that the Taliban are now so fractured that they lack the homogeneity to have a common ideology, how can coalition forces combat the threat using a counterinsurgency strategy? The simple answer is, they cannot. Instead, a new strategy focused on law enforcement would better address these international criminal organizations.

In Afghanistan and across the border in Pakistan, the recruitment of fighters is relatively easy given the lack of opportunity and prosperity for young Muslim males. This disenchanted population is further exacerbated by the warrior mentality which permeates Pashtun tribes. The old adage of "move to the sound of the guns" is very real to these tribes and many become "accidental insurgents" who sometimes participate in battles initiated by the Taliban because it would simply violate their honor not to join in an attack on a foreign force.[30]   In November 2007, one of the author's patrols traveling in

---

[28] Metz, *Rethinking Insurgency,* 9-10.

[29] Meredith, Villarreal, and Wilkinson, "Afghanistan: The De-evolution of Insurgency," 10.

[30] David Killcullen, *The Accidental Guerrilla* (New York: Oxford University Press, 2009): 40.

the narrow Jalrez Valley in Wardak Province experienced just this type of opportunity attack. After conducting a *shura* at a local police station, a four vehicle convoy was struck and pinned down by relentless rocket propelled grenade (RPG), machine gun and small arms fire. Two additional patrols were sent ten kilometers into the valley to assist and the unit received continuous fire while moving more than five kilometers out of the valley. While the Taliban had initiated the initial attack, locals had lined the valley floor to participate in the biggest thing that had happened in the valley in most of their lives. Two U.S. armored high mobility multi-wheeled vehicles were totally destroyed and left at the scene and eight U.S. soldiers were injured, two of them seriously. Despite sympathy for some of its ideas, the Taliban and Al Qaeda do not enjoy broad support throughout Afghanistan because of their harsh tactics and their strict ideology. Even so, Pashtun warriors will pick up arms and fight even if they do not share the same political views as the insurgents.

Recent research further shows that "terrorists groups that kill civilians seldom accomplish their strategic goals," yet the Taliban continues to kill civilians with increasing regularity.[31] The United Nations Assistance Mission Afghanistan (UNAMA) reported that 2009 civilian deaths (5,978) were a fourteen percent increase over 2008 and the most in the war so far. Further, that most of those casualties (sixty-seven percent) were caused by insurgent attacks, many of them from improvised explosive devices and from suicide attacks.[32] While the 2010 civilian casualty numbers are still being

---

[31] National Intelligence Council, *Global Trends 2025: A Transformed World* (Washington DC: US Government Printing Office, November 2008), 69.

[32] UNAMA, "Afghanistan: Annual Report on Protection of Civilians in Armed Conflict," http://unama.unmissions.org/Portals/UNAMA/human%20rights/Protection%20of%20Civilian%202009%20report%20English.pdf (accessed on November 19, 2010).

validated, they regrettably show a further overall increase and in those caused by insurgents. Regardless, the combination of the "warrior" mentality along with high unemployment, poverty, and limited opportunity produces a healthy reserve of insurgent recruits as well as opportunity insurgents.

Recent Events in Afghanistan

In February 2010, U.S. and coalition forces working together under the International Security Assistance Forces (ISAF) banner, initiated a large scale military intervention of a Taliban stronghold in the city of Marjeh (also spelled Marja and Marjah). This attack in the southern province of Helmand in the southern Afghan desert was promoted by General McCrystal as an example of how ISAF was going to reverse the Taliban comeback across the country and begin to reestablish the rule of law and governance. While the initial military attack was wildly successful and caught many Taliban leaders by surprise, various realities soon began to offer a more sobering assessment of the mission dubbed OPERATION MOSHTARAK. With overwhelming force, ISAF along with their Afghan National Army (ANA) and Afghan National Police (ANP) partners converged on Marjeh from helicopters and on the ground causing many Taliban leaders and fighters to flee. Within two weeks, the area was largely secure as road construction began and police stations were established despite some sporadic resistance and pervasive roadside bombs. Unfortunately, the "government in a box" promised by ISAF failed to materialize and while some markets re-opened, essential services were still ineffective at serving the population and now, months after the operation that was promoted as the "tipping point" for this influential province, two battalions of Marines remain in Marjeh while returning Taliban still "spread messages of terror at night and plant bombs that kill Marines and villagers."[33] Despite effective raids that have focused on mid-level Taliban leaders throughout southern Afghanistan and particularly in Helmand, the Taliban leadership has been quick to highlight ISAF operations in Marjeh as an embarrassing defeat. Taliban spokesman Qari Yousef Ahmadi boasted that despite thousands of coalition and Afghan soldier's efforts, Taliban influence was "expanding" in the area and that western forces are now "ashamed to even mention the name of Marjeh, due to their disgraceful defeat."[34]

Many of the failures to achieve stability in Marjeh after the successful accomplishment of the initial military objectives were a result of the inability of Afghans to work and live within a centralized system of government and similarly their lack of competence to provide leadership and services beyond the local or tribal level. It is one of the essential paradoxes of conflict in Afghanistan that the more effort Western nations put into the establishment of a legitimate, strong, and centralized government, the less stability is actually created and the more influence the insurgency gains. In fact, stability in Afghanistan has been decreasing since 2005, due as much to a resurgent Taliban as to government corruption and ineffectiveness. The evidence further shows that developmental assistance in Afghanistan has not convincingly contributed to short-term stability.[35] Polls conducted by the International Council on Security and Development questioning four hundred Afghan males in Marjeh and in neighboring villages after OPERATION MOSHTARAK revealed that sixty-one percent now felt "more negative"

---

[33] Tony Perry, "Buckling Down in Helmand, Marines are thinking long-haul for fight for the Afghan province," *The Los Angeles Times*, August 28, 2010, A1.

[34] Ibid.

[35] Thomas Blau and Daryl Liskey, "Analytics and Action in Afghanistan," *Prism*, Volume 1, No. 4 (September 2010): 49-50.

about Western forces and ISAF, ninety-five percent felt that "more young Afghans will join the Taliban" because of the operation, and finally fifty-nine percent felt that the "Taliban would return to Marjeh after the operation."[36]

While the operation in Marjeh was supposed to focus on helping the Afghan people and promoting the classical COIN mantra of winning the hearts and minds, the reality was an ineffective operation that did not emphasize enough effective local government training and support and instead focused too heavily on military force. As operations for a similar thrust into Kandahar are ongoing, some of these lessons are already being considered. Finding the right balance between military actions, aid/development and governance assistance at the local level will be the key to ensuring that the offensive into Kandahar does not also become another propaganda tool for the Taliban.

---

[36] Alexander Jackson, "Operation Moshtarak: Lessons Learned," *International Council on Security and Development*, http://www.icosgroup.net/modules/reports/operation_moshtarak, (accessed December 4, 2010).

CHAPTER 4
RECOMMENDED CHANGES FOR CONTEMPORARY COUNTERINSURGENCY

In order to make comprehensive and actionable recommendations for changing classical counterinsurgency (COIN) to address contemporary challenges imposed by today's complex security environment and globally networked insurgents, it is necessary to consider both the strategy of when and how to engage in this form of irregular warfare and also the doctrine used to direct activity on the ground. Thus far, this paper has examined the current thinking of U.S. national security leaders and their decision to support the ongoing COIN conflict in Afghanistan as well as a review of the supporters and detractors of the current doctrine espoused in Army Field Manual (FM) 3-24. The current situation in Afghanistan was then detailed to expose it as a worst case or most dangerous environment in which to successfully conduct COIN. Now, based on this critical review and the author's experience from more than thirty months of cumulative time spent directly supporting the COIN fight in Afghanistan, changes will be proposed with the intent to rethink our overall strategy for how and when a COIN campaign is prudent and further, what changes should be implemented in the next edition of FM 3-24.

In terms of a COIN strategy from which to wage irregular war against insurgents trying to impose their will against a government that the U.S. considers a partner, several considerations should be addressed from the outset before military force is considered. The current struggle in Afghanistan provides an excellent example to showcase the challenge of determining the center of gravity and the metrics from which to determine the desired military end state in an unconventional war. This challenge becomes even more daunting if the fight for Afghanistan is considered as but one theater in a global insurgency. U.S. national security leaders need to spend the time to frame this strategy as a part of a grand strategy that has eluded the nation since National Security Council Resolution 68 which guided the U.S. through the end of the Cold War. Without such clear guidance, which should include classified resourcing details, America risks an unfocused and therefore ineffective approach to the global jihad which has been loosely described as the ongoing conflict between liberal democracies and militant Islam. Like the 1953 Project Solarium Conference directed by President Eisenhower, a similar senior level national security planning effort is now required to establish the centers of gravity along with the desired objectives for this ongoing conflict so that we can effectively allocate diminishing resources.

This is particularly important in COIN because it can be argued that there are multiple centers of gravity that insurgents and counterinsurgents fight to influence. While Clausewitz might contend that each center of gravity needs to receive equal effort and resources, the unfortunate reality imposed by constrained resources is that these centers of gravity need to be prioritized. If the Taliban sanctuary in Pakistan, Taliban leadership, ideology, lines of communication, sustainment, command and control and funding sources are considered valid centers of gravity the U.S. and coalition forces must influence in Afghanistan, then is it realistic to think that all of these can be influenced simultaneously and equally? This is even more problematic while expending resources to defend the friendly centers of gravity including the legitimacy of the Karzai government, international support and the will of the people (the one professed continually by classical COIN experts as winning the heart and minds of the population). By analyzing and prioritizing critical capabilities and critical vulnerabilities, however, these centers of gravity can be more appropriately ranked and then appropriately resourced. While this type of analysis must be conducted by national security experts, it must also involve a whole of government review to ensure that all the elements of national power (Diplomatic, Economic, Military, and Information) are considered and that unity of purpose and unity of effort are achieved. If the strategic framework is established to defeat the global jihad, like it was for the Cold War, the U.S. will be better oriented when considering the resources and time required for entering a COIN fight prior to the deployment of troops or the engagement of any of the other instruments of national power. Further, equipped with these guidelines national leaders will be better able to decide if the insurgency demands a response and if so, what type of response. As no two insurgencies are the same, each must be fully examined to determine if it meets the criteria of threatening vital U.S. national security interests. Clearly, not all insurgencies are related or connected to the global insurgency being promoted by Islamic fundamentalists; however, those that do are potentially more threatening.

Steven Metz argues that the distinctive insurgent settings that warrant specific levels of U.S. response should be based on the degree to which a "functioning government" exists and the existence of an "international or regional consensus for the formation of a neo-trusteeship."[1] A simpler and more prudent model may be to link all U.S. actions involving any element of national power to the previously mentioned (and still forthcoming) grand strategy to position America to defeat the global jihad. If an insurgency anywhere in the world threatens vital national interests through transnational terrorism, the U.S. must fully examine the security environment, the culture, the

---

[1] Metz, *Rethinking Insurgency*, 56.

41

legitimacy of the existing government, the level of international support, and the ties the insurgency has to other insurgent groups. In some cases, where the insurgents are isolated (not networked with global jihadists, not receiving significant support from outside sources and not a threat to vital U.S. interests), the U.S. response should be limited to simple over watch and containment. On the other hand, any variation of more threatening options needs to be addressed from a whole of government approach which should be initiated to influence prioritized centers of gravity to best defeat the insurgency and restore stability to the region. Direct COIN support, particularly involving uninvited military intervention, must only be considered in the most threatening situations. When this decision is made, it needs to be properly resourced from the start rather than through a piecemeal escalation (i.e. Vietnam and the policy of Escalated Response) that only protracts the conflict and plays into the hands of the insurgents.

As the U.S. is beginning to realize in Afghanistan, another important consideration in deciding whether or not to undertake COIN support must involve the legitimacy of the supported government in the eyes of its population and the international community. It may be more judicious to serve as a neutral mediator when a government, such as the Karzai Regime in Kabul, has very little credibility outside the capital. This is particularly true when it is not clear that the supported government shares the same end state and objectives as the United States. Much of President Karzai's power in Afghanistan is directly related to the continued presence of Western troops. Propping up a deeply flawed partner in the face of endemic corruption plays into the ideology and propaganda of the insurgents even when the insurgents (like the Taliban) do not enjoy widespread support from the population.

Doctrinally, there are several lessons learned from Afghanistan that have widespread application to other counterinsurgencies and they should be considered in the next update to FM-3-24. Many of these lessons learned challenge the idea that winning the hearts and minds of the population has to be the primary effort of COIN, especially if Afghanistan is considered simply a regional theater of operation in a global jihad loosely organized and sponsored by Al Qaeda and its affiliates such as the Taliban. Traditional or classical COIN techniques are important in understanding how insurgents attempt to impose their will on a government or a population; however, these techniques need to be adjusted in order to defeat a transnational insurgency with modern advantages such as computers, cell phones and the internet.

First and perhaps most importantly, COIN doctrine needs to more fully highlight the trend away from simple cultural awareness, through cultural understanding on the path to cultural appreciation as a requirement for soldiers and civilian leaders at the tactical and operational level. Cultural appreciation is the ability to understand and assess the effects of history, ideology, politics, values, and other cultural dimensions of a region on policy and strategy and it is critical to success in counterinsurgency. The imperative to acquire cultural appreciation requires that the military reach out to civilian experts for assistance as quickly as possible. The recent initiative from the Army's Training and Doctrine Command called the Human Terrain System (HTS) is one such program that helps provide troops with the cultural insight they need to be more effective. Since 2007, these five to nine person teams with experts in social science, anthropology and cultural affairs have been imbedded with various U.S. and NATO forces in the field in Afghanistan where they report the most up to date information to databases for others to use. Although academics have been skeptical and some military leaders have called the initiative a waste of money, the ability of these teams to provide relevant information to commanders in the field has proved successful. The HTS team that was fielded in the author's area of operations in eastern Afghanistan in 2007 influenced a reduction in required combat operations by sixty percent over the first six months of action. Now "there are more than thirty HTS teams in the field with a budget of $150 million."[2] The combination of these embedded experts, better pre-deployment training with culturally accurate role players and the purposeful rotation of specific units back to areas they occupied in previous deployments can all help reduce the cultural divide that can and does impact the effectiveness of counterinsurgency forces.

Another new program instituted by the Chairman of Joint Chiefs of Staff, Admiral Mike Mullen in 2010 is the AfPak (Afghanistan-Pakistan) Hands Program. This initiative involves a complete language and cultural immersion by a select group of military and civilian leaders with a variety of specialized skills (governance, engineering, intelligence, finance, and force protection) who will deploy to Afghanistan and Pakistan and serve as mentors to these host governments and militaries. Because of the U.S. role as the declining sole superpower in an increasingly multi-polar world, insurgencies will continue to thrive as previously suppressed groups seek independence and identity. Cultural appreciation as a part of COIN will therefore continue to be essential in order to successfully maneuver across all three levels of war (strategic, operational, and tactical) and must be better detailed in the update of FM 3-24. The current population-centric focus of FM 3-24 is not capable of addressing the cultural vulnerabilities with which the

---

[2] Joanne Kimberlin, "New Weapon in an Old War," *The Virginian Pilot*, September 26, 2010, 7.

U.S. military can use to fracture the Taliban such that they can no longer destabilize Afghanistan.

An additional shortcoming in the current COIN manual which requires redress involves the limited guidance it provides to the force involving the information operations and how to win the all-important battle of perceptions. FM 3-24 does claim the information environment is "critical" and that the "interconnectedness" of today's insurgents represents a new threat, but it fails to offer any supporting guidance.[3] While insurgents in most unconventional wars will have the advantage of a better understanding of how to communicate with the indigenous population than will the invited foreign forces, the idea of a proactive and offensive information operations effort that is designed to counter those strengths and exploit weaknesses in insurgent messaging must be further developed.

In Afghanistan, the Taliban have been able to effectively disseminate their messages through the timely release of inaccurate and politically charged rhetoric (via press releases and cell phones) and through the destruction they inflict. One offensive information operations campaign the author oversaw did reverse the Taliban's continuous attempts to fabricate allegations that ISAF troops were desecrating the Holy Quran. Despite the lack of any evidence, the story quickly spread and caused riots and violence in several large cities including Kabul and Jalalabad. To counter these untruthful and damaging claims ISAF engaged the population through regionally respected Afghan National Army (ANA) religious leaders. In early 2010, the 201st ANA Corps Mullah was

---

[3] Army Field Manual 3-24, 1-3,1 4.

45

able to visit the site of the alleged Holy Quran desecration with local religious leaders and was able to immediately discredit the allegations. Further, because the evidence showed that the insurgents had actually burned the Holy Quran in an attempt to implicate ISAF, the Mullah was able to reverse the intended effect on the population in several villages and convince them that the Taliban did not share their values. Tactically and operationally, it was the direct messaging provided by competent and uncorrupt Afghans that proved most effective in countering the deceitful message of the Taliban.

The Taliban, like many regional insurgents, lack the reach and influence in information operations that is offered by their Al Qaeda supporters. Their message is primarily based in fear and violence. The U.S. and its allies can counter this message by coordinating messaging with host government and in some cases, the international community. Furthermore, in this and future COIN operations, the U.S. needs to gain and maintain the initiative in information operations by exploiting contradictions in insurgent rhetoric and forcing the insurgents into the dialogue of political discourse vice terror. In Afghanistan, the Taliban have never offered a clear vision of how they will rule or how they will solve the many problems that face the Afghan people. This lack of a plan for the future (politics, reconstruction, education, employment, economics, and human rights) is but one of many insurgent weaknesses that can be exploited. By encouraging the insurgents to explain themselves, they are also moved closer to a political solution and potentially away from violence.

A revised FM 3-24 needs to offer detailed guidance on how to respond to insurgent information operations and how best to exercise initiative in this instantaneous battle of perceptions. Just as the modern insurgent has become so adept at using the international media to spread messages supporting the global jihad, so too, must U.S. military and civilian leaders understand that the media is not necessarily a friend or foe, but rather an uncaring entity which can be manipulated to influence the perceptions of the enemy, neutrals, friends and allies alike. Additionally, the recent government and military aversion to messaging to the domestic audience must be revisited. Propaganda need not be reintroduced in the same jingoistic way that it was during World War II; however, subtle and factual information needs to be professionally fed to the American public if they are expected to continue to expend their limited tax dollars on a protracted and expensive COIN struggle that some believe has limited strategic value.

Another significant omission to current COIN doctrine is the lack of guidance it provides commanders and their staffs on how to recognize and then exploit the organizational structure of insurgent organizations. The current FM 3-24 offers a good example of the Maoist model and also provides some guidance on analyzing other more modern social networks, but it does not provide a detailed framework that both policy makers and military planners need to classify and recommend action against the wide range of loosely networked insurgent groups that have become a part of today's evolving environment. Whether the insurgent organization is Al Qaeda and their transnational affiliates, criminal entities, former paramilitary forces, clans, or the tribal organizational structure previously described involving the Pashtuns in Afghanistan, in order for COIN doctrine to be effective, it needs to provide a way to model these organizations and classify them by their organizational structure, command and control methods, strategic goals, recruiting techniques and operational procedures.

A starting point for the revision of the next FM 3-24 is the model proposed by Abdulkader Sinno in Appendix C. Sinno contends that good choices made by planners at the strategic and operational level of war based on a complete understanding of the organizational structure of the insurgent force can offer the U.S. measurable advantages against asymmetric insurgents.[4] Even the greatly disseminated yet closely networked structure of Al Qaeda has internal fissures, discrepancies and weaknesses that can be targeted. The revised FM 3-24 also needs to provide a framework that can offer commanders and planners a menu of operational approaches based on a more complete understanding of the organizational structure of the targeted insurgent force.

Another oversight from FM 3-24's classical doctrine involves the transnational nature of many modern insurgencies which have been defined by some defense experts as separate campaigns in a worldwide insurgency. Today's global Salafist Islamic insurgents seek to exploit the "fault lines" in what Samuel Huntington describes as the "clash of civilizations" between Islam and the West in order to create a modern pan-Islamic Caliphate and overthrow the West through insurgency, subversion and terrorism.[5] As an essential part of this effort, fundamentalist Islamic ideology and religion around the globe are becoming increasingly radicalized and this weakens the ability of many fragile governments like Yemen and Somalia to provide security, stability and prosperity for their populations. FM 3-24 devotes only a single paragraph to these critical changes to the strategic environment and more guidance is necessary in the revision. The "clear,

---

[4] Sinno, *Organizations at War in Afghanistan and Beyond*, 303-304.

[5] Samuel P. Hunttington, *The Clash of Civilization and the Remaking of the World Order* (New York: Simon and Schuster, 1996). Political scientist Samuel P. Huntington asserts that conflict in the post-Cold War world will primarily be caused by differences in culture and religion and will be exposed on the fault lines between these civilizations.

hold, and build" COIN model outlined by General Petraeus for Afghanistan in Appendix D is simply not a sufficient doctrine to deal with a larger global insurgency, even if this worldwide insurgency is only loosely coordinated.

A more comprehensive FM 3-24 must address the transnational nature of global insurgencies, it must recognize that every insurgency is distinctive and that the population may not always be the prize, and it must address the issue of political legitimacy in insurgency. While the transnational organizational structure of the contemporary insurgent has already been addressed as a shortcoming for the current doctrine, the plethora of other actors in the battlespace of contemporary COIN conflicts also begs attention and direction. The exponential increase in the number of new nation states, nongovernmental agencies, intergovernmental organizations, private relief organizations, and private security organization have cluttered the operational environment today the way Galula and Thompson did not encounter and could never have imagined. A revised FM 3-24 must offer future COIN practitioners some ideas on how to achieve unity of purpose and if possible, unity of effort in this increasingly complex landscape with so many competing special interests.

The recognition of the distinctive characteristics of each insurgency and therefore the requirement for a uniquely tailored COIN strategy to combat each insurgency makes overgeneralized COIN doctrine obsolete. It is the uniqueness of each COIN strategy that needs to be captured in the revised FM 3-24 so that leaders and planners appreciate that no "Jominian" cookbook approach will be effective in fighting an insurgency. Furthermore, the classicist centerpiece argument that the population is the single center of gravity for both the insurgent and the counterinsurgent demands rethinking. This is especially important in an international insurgency where the people may not be relevant if they can be marginalized through violence and intimidation to remain neutral. Most independent surveys of Afghans in various parts of the country view the Taliban and Al Qaeda as criminals as opposed to freedom fighters, yet they continue to exact considerable influence through violence and terror.

The idea that Westerners can ever win the "hearts and minds" in a culture that has value systems and beliefs that are directly opposed to Western culture is futile. Instead, the U.S. and its coalition partners need to realize the systems and values that are effective in a given culture and develop strategies to assist in stability as a truthful broker between the insurgents and a credible government. In Afghanistan, as Major Gant suggests, empowering the traditional powerbrokers (the tribes) can produce positive results. The U.S. choice of a corrupt and ineffective partner in the Karzai Government forced many Afghans to side with the Taliban before they even had any contact with a single U.S. or coalition soldier or civilian. A revised FM 3-24 needs to highlight the importance of adapting COIN methodology depending on the legitimacy of the host government and the congruence of shared U.S. values. The classic democratic, market-based tactic fixated on individual rights has so far proved useless on cultures mired in the thirteenth century.

The last significant improvement to the 2006 Counterinsurgency manual should be the inclusion of an important discussion of the religious influence on insurgencies which is almost wholly omitted. Despite vague references in the introduction to religion as a part of identity and religious extremism as a modern day influence on insurgents, the manual fails to offer any guidance on how COIN must be altered to be more effective against religiously-based insurgent groups. This omission is disturbing considering two important historical facts. First; over the course of human history, the number of people killed and the amount of treasure expended in the name of religious conflict is huge and continues to grow every day. While the current fight is between Islam and Christianity, history is wrought with other similarly destructive examples. Second; nearly half of the world's active terrorists groups today have been classified as religious whereas a generation ago, none were.[6] Furthermore, the vast majority of the contemporary insurgencies that are associated with the mobilization of Muslims as a part of a global insurgency are most certainly inspired by religion.

By not addressing an approach to this serious issue, FM 3-24 leaves planners and commanders unprepared to fight a global insurgency. The revised COIN manual should offer several different approaches that can be applied regardless of the particular religion involved, but also one that will affect the ongoing conflict between militant Islam and liberal democracies. One such approach is the combination of better cultural awareness training for deploying troops and an information operations effort designed to promulgate the idea that the U.S. and its allies are not fighting against greater Islam, but instead only the violent, radicalized elements within the Muslim world. Specific training should involve training on the pillars of the Islamic faith and an overview of the Holy Quran. A specific theme in the information operations campaign must reach out to Islamic leaders to detail the growing number of Muslims that live peacefully throughout America and the rest of the world.

While these recommendations are not all-inclusive, they do address some of the major shortfalls of the current version of FM 3-24 and they can serve as a guidepost to

---

[6] Bruce Hoffman, *Inside Terrorism* (New York: Columbia University Press, 2006), 84-86.

drive ongoing revisions to this important doctrinal tool for the future of human conflict.

To test their applicability to a future conflict, the recommendations will be extrapolated

on the emerging insurgency led by Al-Shabaab in the failed nation-state of Somalia.

CHAPTER 5
SOMALIA CASE STUDY

Somalia, Yemen, the Maghreb, and the Sahel are all listed as areas and countries that are considered "at risk" of becoming failed states in the 2010 *National Security Strategy*. Somalia, however, has already proven so unstable that it has become a safe haven for Al Qaeda (through its relationship with the Al-Shabaab insurgency) and the piracy extending from its shores threatens free trade and prosperity to all those who must transit the Gulf of Aden.[1] Even more ominous to homeland security was the recent planned terrorist attack that was thwarted by the Federal Bureau of Investigation in Portland, Oregon when a Somali born U.S. teenager planned to bomb a crowded Christmas tree-lighting ceremony. This is especially disturbing considering fourteen Somali immigrants (representing only a small portion of the tens of thousands of Somalis that have resettled in America since 1991) were indicted in August 2010 for routing both money and fighters to Al-Shabaab insurgents.[2] Further, after Al-Shabaab took credit for the twin bombings in Kampala, Uganda, President Obama described Somalia as a "breeding ground for terrorism" that must be addressed so that Al-Shabaab cannot continue to "export violence."[3]

The hasty retreat of the United Nations and the U.S. in 1995 (caused largely by the widely publicized deaths of eighteen soldiers in a fierce battle with clans loyal to

---

[1] *National Security Strategy* , 21.

[2] Associated Press, "Oregon Bomb Suspect Wanted 'Spectacular Show,'" http://www.msnbc.msn.com/id/40389899/ns/us news-security/ (assessed November, 28 2010).

[3] President Barrack Obama, interview by the South African Broadcasting Corporation, July 13, 2010, Obama Remarks on Uganda, African Terroism, http://www.white house.gov/the-press-office/interview-president-south-african-broadcasting-corporation (accessed on December 17, 2010).

Mohamed Farrah Aidid which occurred in October 1993) may make it less likely that the U.S. will again commit the military into direct action in Somalia. On the other hand, the rapidly deteriorating situation there now may soon directly affect our vital national security interests in a way that will make the international pressure that coerced the American and United Nations intervention there in the 1990s seem insignificant.

Counterinsurgency (COIN) in Somalia is a daunting proposition that would most likely have to be initiated with hard-power (relying on the military instrument of national power) simply because the U.S. has had little contact with governmental authorities in Somalia. Diplomatic and economic instruments of power in Somalia may not be practical at the onset. The informational instrument of power, however, may provide another opportunity for engagement as Somalia is one of Africa's fastest growing mobile communications markets. While the threats that a lawless, ungoverned Somalia pose to the U.S. and the world are real and growing, a purely military response will likely only offer short term results. Improvements to governance and the economy along with a comprehensive whole of government strategy to address the inequities in wealth and power in Somalia are necessary if the U.S. is to be successful in providing stability to ungoverned spaces like this that present a direct risk to national security. The proposed revisions to the U.S. Army Counterinsurgency Manual may not guarantee success in Somalia's complicated security environment; however, the effective employment of these revisions should avoid the pitfalls that have led to the protracted and still undecided conflict in Afghanistan.

First, as in the case of the Afghanistan case study, it is necessary to understand the nature of the security environment in Somalia with regard to geography, history and culture. This review will require less detail than the Afghanistan case study because unlike the Taliban movement and its close ties to the Pashtun warrior culture, the influence of Al-Shabaab in Somalia is a relatively new occurrence. The Al-Shabaab ideology is also a foreign phenomenon that has been imported rather than developed internally over centuries. With a thorough understanding of the security environment especially in the wake of current events, it is easy to hypothesize how Somalia, like Afghanistan, could quickly become the next focus of a counterinsurgency (COIN) operation.

Historical Background

Named after the legendary father of the Somali people, *Samaal*, Somalia is an arid country in the Horn of Africa that is slightly smaller than the State of Texas. Just to the east of Ethiopia, Somalia borders both the Gulf of Aden and the Indian Ocean with over 1,800 miles of coastline; see the map in Appendix E. As a result of its desert climate, over-grazing and minimal arable lands, famine and drought have combined with political instability to make Somalia the world's leading "at risk" state based on the Failed State Index (FSI) compiled by the Fund for Peace who annually rates countries throughout the world using twelve detailed indicators of stability.[4] Somali society is clan based and vaguely similar to the tribal social structure previously described in Afghanistan. Clans have prevailed in Somalia since the twelfth century which is coincidentally when Islam was introduced in the region.

---

[4] The Fund for Peace, "Failed States Index 2010," http://www.fundforpeace.org/web/index.php?option=com_content&task=view&id=99&Itemid=140 (accessed on January 6, 2011).

In the nineteenth century, Somalia was split between four colonial powers: England, France, Italy and Ethiopia. Finally, in 1949 the nation became a United Nations trust territory until its independence as a democratic state in 1960. A variety of internal conflicts triggered a civil war in 1990 and ever since the nation has struggled with lawlessness, chaos and famine. Currently, Somalia is made up of three semi-autonomous regions: Somalia proper, Puntland, and Somaliland. While Puntland and Somaliland currently operate independently, they have both expressed a desire to reintegrate into greater Somalia once a stable government is reestablished. Currently, the government in Somalia is a fragile Transitional Federal Government (TFG). The TFG is the fourteenth attempt to create a functioning government in Somalia since the end of Muhammad Siad Barre's dictatorial rule in 1991 and is the product of several years of international mediation led by the Intergovernmental Authority on Development.[5]

Somali Clan Culture

One of the most ethnically and culturally homogeneous countries in Africa, Somalis make up eighty-five percent of the population which also includes minority Arabs, Southeast Asians and Bantus. Except for the often persecuted Bantus, most Somalis share a common language, faith and cultural norms. Patrilineal clans and sub clans make up the societal structure and serve as a source of solidarity in that they provide for protection and access to resources, but also a source of conflict in that unstable alliances between clans cause struggles for power and influence. Like the tribes in Afghanistan, the clan in Somalia commonly outweighs any allegiance to the country. Nationalism is not a consideration for the average Somali and the clan, after the male-

---

[5] *The World Factbook.*

dominated family, is the most important and most basic social organization.[6] Also

similar to the Pashtun tribes of Afghanistan is the permeation of the warrior culture

throughout Somali society where a state of perpetual conflict exists either between

Somalia and the outside world, between the clans within Somalia, or even brother against

brother in a Somali family.

Another similarity to Afghan culture is the increasingly strict adherence to Islamic

cultural traditions including the separation of genders in public, the covering of women in

public from head to toe, and unfortunately female subjugation which in Somalia also

takes the form of genital mutilation or circumcision which is endured by ninety-eight

percent of Somali women.[7] Somalis are Sunni Muslims and their faith influences almost

all of their cultural norms, attitudes and practices. The transition to strict interpretation of

Islamic Law and customs is a relatively recent (1990s) and appears to be a foreign

inspired concept. Again, while Islam spread to the region around 1100 A.D., the more

fundamentalist practices seen today including amputation sentences for thefts and death

sentences by public stoning for adultery have been imported from other Islamic

fundamentalists in areas controlled by Al-Shabaab insurgents.[8]

---

[6] Centers for Disease Control and Prevention, "Overview of Somali Culture," in *Promoting Cultural Sensitivity : A Practical Guide for Tuberculosis Programs That Provide Services to Persons from Somalia.* http://www.cdc.gov/tb/publications/guidestoolkits/EthnographicGuides/Somalia/default.htm (assessed January 7, 2011).

[7] United States Department of State, *Somalia: Report on Female Genital Mutilation (FGM) or Female Genital Cutting (FGC)* (Washington: GPO) http://www.state.gov/g/wi/rls/rep/crfgm/10109pf.htm (accessed January 9, 2011).

[8] *The World Factbook..*

The Ideology of the Al-Shabaab Insurgent

The ideology of Al-Shabaab, like that of other militant groups involved in the global jihad, continues to mutate. Unfortunately, the mutation towards the export of violence to achieve its ends is an unwelcome development for the United States and liberal democracies in the West. Al-Shabaab ideology closely mirrors the dogma championed by both the Taliban and Al Qaeda: the unquestioned adherence to *Sharia* law, the establishment of an Islamic caliphate representing a new world order led by Muslims, and the indiscriminate use of violence to achieve those ends. Reviewing recent public statements made by Al-Shabaab leaders from Al Qaeda's primary media outlet, the Global Islamic Media Foundation (GIMF), it is clear that Al-Shabaab is not only affiliated with Al Qaeda, but it also models its social engineering/population control measures from the Taliban example. [9] It also appears that Al-Shabaab believes it is fighting within the Al Qaeda established framework for the global jihad.

Several recent examples of such "Talibanization" include: the destruction and desecration of non-Muslim places of worship; the banning of cultural activities such as dancing, music and movies; and the elimination of unbelievers, infidels, and deviant Muslims. Although Al-Shabaab's objective to create a Taliban-like Islamic state is not a majority held view among Somalis, the transformation of the Al-Shabaab ideology into practice through these type of social control measures continues to advance. As long as Al-Shabaab's "alien ideology" does not violate closely held Somali cultural norms, it will

---

[9] Michael Taarnby and Lars Hallundbaek, "Somalia: The Internalization of Militant Islam and the Implications for Radicalisation Processes in Europe," http://www.jUStitsministeriet.dk/fileadmin/downloads/Forskning_og_dokumentation/Forskningspulje/Taarnby-rapport.pdf (accessed January 9, 2011), 13.

likely continue to grow and mutate.[10] If it does start to violate traditional Somali culture, popular resistance can be guaranteed.

There are also links to other regional jihadi groups that share similar ideology and affiliation with Al Qaeda. For instance, there has been recent reporting that suggests both personnel and material exchanges along established supply routes between Al-Shabaab and jihadi insurgents in both Yemen and Eritrea. On December 5, 2010 Somali troops reported the death of Rabah Abu-Qalid (a popular Yemini jihadist) in fighting with them in Mogadishu. On November 23, 2010 Yemeni government officials reported that they had arrested several Al-Shabaab insurgents at the al-Kharaz refugee camp in Yemen.[11] Whether or not Islamic insurgent groups like Al-Shabaab in the Horn of Africa (HOA) are full-fledged Al Qaeda members has not been determined conclusively; however, it is clear through internet posting and actions on the ground, that mutual support does exist. In the case of Al-Shabaab, it is also clear that there is an unquestionable desire to become an operational branch of Al Qaeda in Africa.

The implication of this trend toward greater radicalization and greater synchronization in the global jihad threatens U.S. efforts to combat piracy and the export of terror in the region. The question remains; how dangerous does it have to get before the U.S. will have to act in order to protect its vital national security interests? The underwear bomber who attempted to ignite an explosive and bring down a commercial airliner destined for Detroit on Christmas Eve 2010 was allegedly trained and resourced in Yemen. In early February 2011, four American boaters were hijacked by Somali

---

[10] Ibid., Pg, 15.

[11] STRATFOR, "Limited Cooperation Between Somali Militants, Jemeni Jihadists," http://www.stratfor.com/analysis/20101209-limited-cooperation-between-somali-militants-yemini -jihadists (accessed December 17, 2010).

pirates and killed aboard their vessels. The next major attack (when, not if), attempted or successful, could just as easily originate from Somalia. The question U.S. leaders will need to answer given this likely scenario is how the U.S. and its allies will react. This is even more important if direct action is required. The options are too numerous to contemplate. Given our recent experiences in Iraq and Afghanistan and the popularity of COIN among military and civilian defense leaders, it is reasonable to assume that a counterinsurgency operation against Al-Shabaab could be one of the leading options. If this crucial decision to engage in a COIN campaign in Somalia is made, it must be done so with strategic acumen based on realistic end states. Furthermore, it must incorporate some of the aforementioned operational and tactical recommendations that can make this COIN effort compatible with this globally-connected contemporary security environment.

Recommendations for Counterinsurgency in Somalia

The decision to engage in a COIN campaign against Al-Shabaab should not be taken lightly or without the consideration of a detailed campaign design. Even if another watershed event like the Al Qaeda attack on New York and Washington in 2001 occurs and is linked to Somalia, U.S. leaders should avoid the "one size fits all" approach when reacting. While the appetite for immediate revenge will resonate with the American public for a while, these waves of public support tend not to be enduring and are also greatly affected by the election cycle. A COIN strategy, on the other hand, is by its very nature, costly and protracted. Therefore, any COIN operation in Somalia needs to be a part of a larger fight against the global insurgency in the context of the battle between militant Islam and liberal democracy. If it remains unrelated to this contemporary viewpoint and is isolated to a classical irregular war solely against Al-Shabaab within the confines of Somalia, the likelihood of success will be greatly reduced. Instead, it will become a long-drawn-out struggle that will further exhaust our national treasure and play directly into Al Qaeda's plan to economically bleed the West into submission and establish a new world order.

Time and effort needs to be expended now through a President Eisenhower inspired "Project Solarium" Conference to establish a grand strategy for the global jihad. This framework strategy should already be in place prior to reacting to the next attack whether it originates in Somalia or not. The development of a new grand strategy as well as any specific COIN campaign for Somalia must also include a detailed center of gravity (COG) analysis which prioritizes each enemy and friendly COG so that they can be resourced appropriately despite shrinking resources caused by the global economic recession. Even a rudimentary COG analysis of Al-Shabaab reveals several Al Shabaab COGs including: armed insurgent forces, leadership, ideology, lines of communication, funding sources, and command and control. These COGs will have to be prioritized and appropriately resourced in order to defeat Al-Shabaab and reestablish stability in Somalia.

Furthermore, considerations need to be made early in any recommendation for a COIN strategy in Somalia on whether or not there is international support for the effort. Given the threat to shipping caused by piracy originating in Somalia and the recent exportation of terror via the Al-Shabaab orchestrated bombings in Uganda, international support should not be difficult to muster. Regardless, any international effort needs to be unified by purpose and needs to include a coordinated whole of government approach to help alleviate the multitude of problems that affect the average Somali including poverty, drought, famine, and endemic corruption. Steve Metz would likely suggest that due to the current lack of "neo-trusteeship" for a COIN effort in Somalia, a low impact strategy based on over-watch and containment is all that should be initiated. However, the regional and increasingly more international efforts spearheaded by Joint Task Force Horn of Africa and the European Union focused on piracy show that a "neo-trusteeship" may be already be forming. A watershed event could quickly galvanize the current international cooperation around the HOA into a more mature counterinsurgency operation.

Also significant is the critical lesson recently observed in Afghanistan regarding the choice of a partner government with which to collaborate. Led by President Sheikh Sharif Ahmed, the Transitional Federal Government (TFG) in Somalia operates on a mandate that authorizes power through the end of August 2011. Instead, the TFG has voted earlier this year to extend the mandate for three more years. The TFG remains a fledging and fragile government which has struggled since forming in 2004 with the authorization and support of the United Nations. Before the U.S. and its allies throw support to bolster a host government like the TFG, they need to clearly understand its legitimacy among the populace. Right now, supporting President Shariff may be akin to supporting President Karzai in Afghanistan and this may not be the partner we need in order to separate the insurgents from the population. With tenuous control and only limited credibility in portions of the capital, a new legitimate partner government will likely be required in Somalia.

Operationally and tactically, several other adjustments to our current classical

COIN doctrine as detailed in Army Field Manual (FM) 3-24 need to be initiated prior to

any intervention into Somalia, invited or not. First, the issue of understanding and

embracing Somali culture in terms of cultural appreciation vice simple cultural

understanding needs to be instilled in all deploying soldiers and civilians. While the U.S.

and several of its allies have a head start in Somalia from the international experience

there as a part of the 1992 humanitarian mission OPERATION RESTORE HOPE in

support of the United Nations Task Force (UNITAF) and the ill-fated follow-on

peacekeeping operation called United Nations Operation Somalia (UNISOM II) in 1994;

U.S. national security leaders should already be leaning forward to establish the

framework to re-learn the intricacies of Somali culture to improve on this baseline

experience. It will be too late to gain the requisite language and cultural skills if the U.S.

waits until an intervention is necessary. While a program similar to the current AfPak

Hands program may be premature, a less inclusive program should already be planned

and in the execution phase with an emphasis on Special Forces assets. Because of the

homogeneous religious, ethnic and cultural make-up of Somalia, exercising cultural

appreciation early in Somalia can potentially be an even greater combat multiplier than it

has been in the more heterogeneous and fractured cultural landscape of Afghanistan. To

further assist in quickly gaining cultural appreciation, the early addition of the

aforementioned Human Terrain Teams (HTTs) through the Human Terrain System

(HTS) should also be included in any "boots on the ground" direct action.

The second necessary change to FM 3-24 that will enable success for a potential

COIN campaign in Somalia is an offensive-minded information operations (IO) effort designed to gain and maintain the initiative in the critical fight over perceptions: perceptions of Somalis, perceptions of the international community, and domestic perceptions in the United States. This IO effort can and should begin immediately as it is relatively cheap and because the U.S. and the West is already losing this fight in Somalia and in most of the Islamic world. To be offensive in IO, U.S. military and civilian leaders need to commit to a messaging plan (strategically, operationally, and tactically) that is nested in the still forthcoming grand strategy designed to fight the global jihad. The pillars of this messaging plan need to focus on re-characterizing the current struggle as a fight between liberal democracies and only the minority of militant Islamists who wish to use violence to achieve their goals.

The IO plan must also utilize moderate Muslims and other Muslim religious leaders to deliver this message and focus on the deliberate exploitation of the fallacy and shallowness of Al-Shabaab's ideology. Like the Taliban, Al-Shabaab has not and does not offer any tangible solutions to the problems facing most Somalis. Economic opportunity, political reform, infrastructure improvement, and education development are not part of the Al-Shabaab message to the people. This lack of vision for the future of Somalia beyond the mere institution of *Sharia* law and the subjugation of non-believers needs to be exploited. Not only will it cause Somalis to question the direction Al-Shabaab is taking the country, it will also force Al-Shabaab into political discourse and potentially away from violence if they are able to develop credibility among the people without relying on terror and forced social re-engineering that is alien to Somalia.

Understanding the organizational structure of Al-Shabaab is another necessary requirement prior to any planned COIN intervention into Somalia. While the current FM

3-24 offers only a Maoists model for consideration, the use of the model proposed by Abdulkader Sinno in Appendix C, or something similar to it, will provide military and civilian planners the capability to exploit the internal organizational structure of Al-Shabaab and likewise target fractures and fissures in the loosely networked global affiliation of Al Qaeda. With a thorough understanding of the centralized structure of Al-Shabaab and its multiple internal divisions, a menu of approaches can be determined and applied to best focus limited U.S. resources on enemy critical vulnerabilities. Furthermore, by understanding the organizational structure and hierarchy of the clan social system, the U.S. and its allies can make a concerted effort to enable the traditional sources of power in Somalia, rather than blindly empowering the host government. Major Gant's proposal of tribal empowerment as a method to dislodge the Taliban "village by village" in Afghanistan has a similar likelihood of success in Somalia against Al-Shabaab and could be called a "clan by clan" approach.

A final required change from the classical approach to COIN presented in FM 3-24 is the notion each insurgency is unique and therefore every COIN campaign must be customized. The assumption of COIN classicists that the population is the singular center of gravity for both the insurgents and the counterinsurgents must be proven. In Somalia, the recent "talibanization" of society has intimidated the Somalis to support or at least remain neutral to the radical reforms being imposed upon them. In effect, that makes the population less relevant, especially if Al-Shabaab is considered but one front in a global insurgency. Furthermore, the idea that Western nations can intervene without being considered invaders and quickly win the "heart and mind" of the average Somali is ludicrous, especially given our recent history and the fact that our cultures are so dissimilar. Also, the differences in motivation and ideology between the criminally motivated clans responsible for much of the piracy off the Somali coast and that of the fundamentalist Al-Shabaab insurgents must be exploited. Lieutenant Colonel Dennis Larsen proposes a "Phase Zero Stability Operation" to counter the growing piracy problem which involves a hybrid model between COIN and Stability Operations that will harness the capabilities of a whole of government approach to achieve the greatest possible results.[12] Proposals like this deserve immediate consideration and implementation given the deteriorating security situation in Somalia.

In summary, no predetermined recipe for guaranteed success exists for a potential COIN campaign against Al-Shabaab insurgents in Somalia. There are, however, modifications from the current FM 3-24 that will make such an intervention more likely to succeed. While FM 3-24 is still in revision, the lessons learned over the past decade of intense COIN conflict in Afghanistan and Iraq reveal that a contemporary and customized approach must be applied in future irregular warfare against insurgent forces, particularly those that are linked to a wider global effort like Al-Shabaab.

---

[12] Dennis Larson, *Somali Pirates: A New Phase Zero Stability Operational Approach, A Strategic Imperative in the Horn of Africa, Research Paper*, (Norfolk, VA: Joint Forces Staff College, 18 June 2010), 12.

CHAPTER 6
CONCLUSION

While few would argue that Army Field Manual (FM) 3-24, *Counterinsurgency*, was not a valuable advancement in the strategy and doctrine of combatting insurgents in irregular war when it was published in 2006, few also now believe that the classicists viewpoint which pervades the document is wholly relevant in today's complex, globally connected security environment. The 1960s theorists, including David Galula with experience from Algeria and Sir Robert Thompson with experience in Malaysia and other British campaigns, are the pillars of the population centric approach to counterinsurgency (COIN) strategy and doctrine. While one of FM 3-24s authors, John Nagl, concedes that this COIN manual is no "*Bible*" and that it is scheduled for a rewrite within the next year, he also states that those who "decry the doctrine's focus on the population" will be disappointed with the revision.[1] U.S. military and civilian defense leaders should take comfort in the knowledge that the COIN manual is being updated, they should likewise be alarmed that this effort is being conducted by the same talented core of authors who have thus far refused to acknowledge the relevancy of insurgents that are religiously inspired, loosely networked and globally connected. Their level of concern should also be heightened if the revised doctrine does not also stress the importance of fighting an insurgency through a cultural lens that focuses on an appreciation of the host/insurgent culture.

Classical COIN theory establishes the baseline for fighting with and defeating insurgents; however, it cannot in its current state prepare and guide commanders in the

---

[1]Nagl, "Learning to Adapt and Win," 123.

67

field who are pitted against violent fundamentalists who consider their death in the global jihad as the ultimate sacrifice and salvation for all Muslims. While many basic tenets and paradoxes offered in the current manual remain germane (such as "achieving unity of effort," "understanding the environment" and "the more force you use, the less effective you are"), the unabated focus on the population begs re-examination at the highest levels of U.S. leadership.[2] The reason this is so critical is because it causes military and civilian planners to focus on only one center of gravity; the people. This occurs at the expense of other important centers of gravity and is commonly tied to the misguided notion of "winning the hearts of minds" of cultures that are so alien to Western culture that such an objective is simply absurd.

The literature review described the basic principles and paradoxes included in FM 3-24 and then went on to detail several of the most recent critiques of the document. While there are some including Colonel Gian Gentile who argue for the complete "deconstruction" of the doctrine in a methodology similar to what occurred with Active Defense Doctrine from 1976, this proposal is not reasonable given the violent nature of the ongoing conflict and the continued relevancy of major portions of the doctrine as written. On the other hand, other detractors correctly argue that the myopic focus on anti-colonial insurgent conflicts from the 1960s oversimplifies COIN doctrine and strategy such that is fails to account for the contemporary operating environment and more specifically the global nature and religious motivation of militant Islamists.

The Afghanistan case study provided several cogent examples of what can be considered a "worst case" scenario for a COIN strategy to be successful. However, some

---

[2] Army Field Manual 3-24, 1-27, 1-28.

of the suggested changes and additions to FM 3-24 are already having some positive effects as President Obama's troop increase have only recently arrived in total. These additional forces and the continued modifications to the current COIN doctrine have caused several positive developments in the past year including: the Taliban has lost "all of its principle safe havens in the south," Taliban "weapons and equipment" flow has been disrupted, several "local populations have stepped forward to fight the Taliban with ISAF support."[3] On the other hand, for some of the reasons in the case study, there are still major challenges with regard to political reform, corruption, cross-border safe havens in Pakistan, and the professionalism and training of security forces which are causing the war in Afghanistan to be the most protracted conflict in U.S. history.

The recommended changes and additions to the COIN manual were proposed using this worst case scenario in Afghanistan as a framework for discussion. The recommendations are based on experiences at both the tactical and operational levels of war over three different tours of duty from 2003 to 2010. While there are no cookbook solutions for defeating an insurgency, the U.S. and its allies can and should get better and learn from each COIN experience. The key during each conflict is to adapt to changing conditions sooner than the enemy does to maintain the initiative. The U.S. defense establishment is notoriously slow to adapt and so far, our COIN strategy and doctrine has been no exception. The strategic recommendations were twofold. First, the establishment of a grand strategy for the global jihad with early and accurate determinations / prioritizations of enemy and friendly centers of gravity to direct the

---

[3] Frederick Kagan and Kimberly Kagan, *Defining Success in Afghanistan, Executive Summary*, A Report by the American Enterprise Institute and the Institute for the Study of War, 2011, http://aie.org/docLib/DefiningSuccessinAfghanistanElectronicVersion.pdf (accessed on 2 February 2011).

campaign design. Second, the immediate consideration of alternative courses of action in a COIN scenario based on the regional security environment, the culture, the credibility of the host government, the level of international support and the ties the insurgency has to other insurgent groups. Doctrinally, the recommendations focused on embracing cultural appreciation throughout a whole of government approach, gaining and maintaining the initiative in information operations, exploiting the knowledge of the organizational structure of insurgent organizations, recognizing the distinctive transnational nature of contemporary insurgencies and their role in a larger global insurgency, and recognizing the crucial role of religion in contemporary insurgencies.

The final case study on Somalia was designed to test some of the recommendations derived from the case study on Afghanistan and apply them to a deteriorating security situation there which may soon threaten vital U.S. national interests. Al-Shabaab has taken the Taliban playbook and is exacting its directives through fear and intimidation. Further, it has started to export terror through the recent bombings in Uganda. While the application of some of the recommended changes to FM 3-24 will not guarantee success in any future intervention in Somalia, they will help the U.S. and its allies to avoid many of the pitfalls which have plagued the COIN effort in Afghanistan and even in Iraq. Although the application of these recommendations to Somalia were purely hypothetical, the application and continued modification of COIN strategy and doctrine to each unique insurgent threat will ultimately be required if the United States expects to protect its vital national interests through the duration of this enduring battle against this increasingly global insurgency.

In conclusion, the revision to FM 3-24 is already overdue. The complex security environment facing the United States and coalition forces in Afghanistan and the U.S. reliance on classical counterinsurgency (COIN) doctrine over the past decade has resulted in a costly and protracted conflict whose outcome still remains undetermined. As a result of the lessons learned since FM 3-24 was published, the United States must rethink, revise, and now apply a revised COIN strategy and doctrine including the recommendations herein in order to meet contemporary and future challenges that will satisfy U.S. national security objectives. Nevertheless, the most important and enduring imperative of FM 3-24 still remains – adapt more quickly than the enemy and never stop learning.

APPENDIX B
The *Pashtunwali* Code

The Code of Pashtunwali: The rules listed below have guided Pashtun tribesmen for centuries.

Badal refers to the right to retaliate if insulted.

Badragha is the safe escort of a fugitive or a visitor to his destination.

Balandra is the act of providing help to someone who is unable to complete his own work, such as a harvest. Repayment is usually a lavish dinner.

Baramta is the holding of hostages until claimed property is returned; service industry workers (tailors, barbers, etc.) are excluded from being taken hostage.

Bota is the seizing of property to ensure repayment of debt.

Ghundi is an alliance created against a common enemy.

Hamsaya refers to a man who has given his valuables to someone (usually an elder of another village) who can protect him from insult or injury.

Itbar is the trust in one's word or promise as a legally binding contract.

Lashkar is a large group of armed men who enforce the ruling of a jirga, much like a police and military force would.

Lokhay Warkawal is the acceptance of an alliance in order to gain protection from enemies.

Meerata is the murder of one male member of a family by another in order to ensure inheritance. This is a criminal act and the Jirga responds by punishing the culprit.

Melmastia is generous hospitality, and Pashtuns consider it one of their finest virtues.

Mla Tarr is the provision of armed protection to help a family member or a close friend.

Nanewatei is the act of forgiveness or the grant of asylum, even to enemies. It is not accepted where the honor of a woman is involved.

Saz is "blood money" or other compensation (such as a daughter in marriage) given to appease a family after a murder.

Tarr is an agreement that gives protection to the involved parties.

Teega means literally "putting down the stone" and stands for ending the fighting between two feuding parties.

Tor is disgrace through extramarital or premarital sex (or rape) and is punishable by death.

(https://ronna-afghan.harmonieweb.org/Pages/*Pashtunwali*.aspx)

APPENDIX C
Organizational Structure Theory

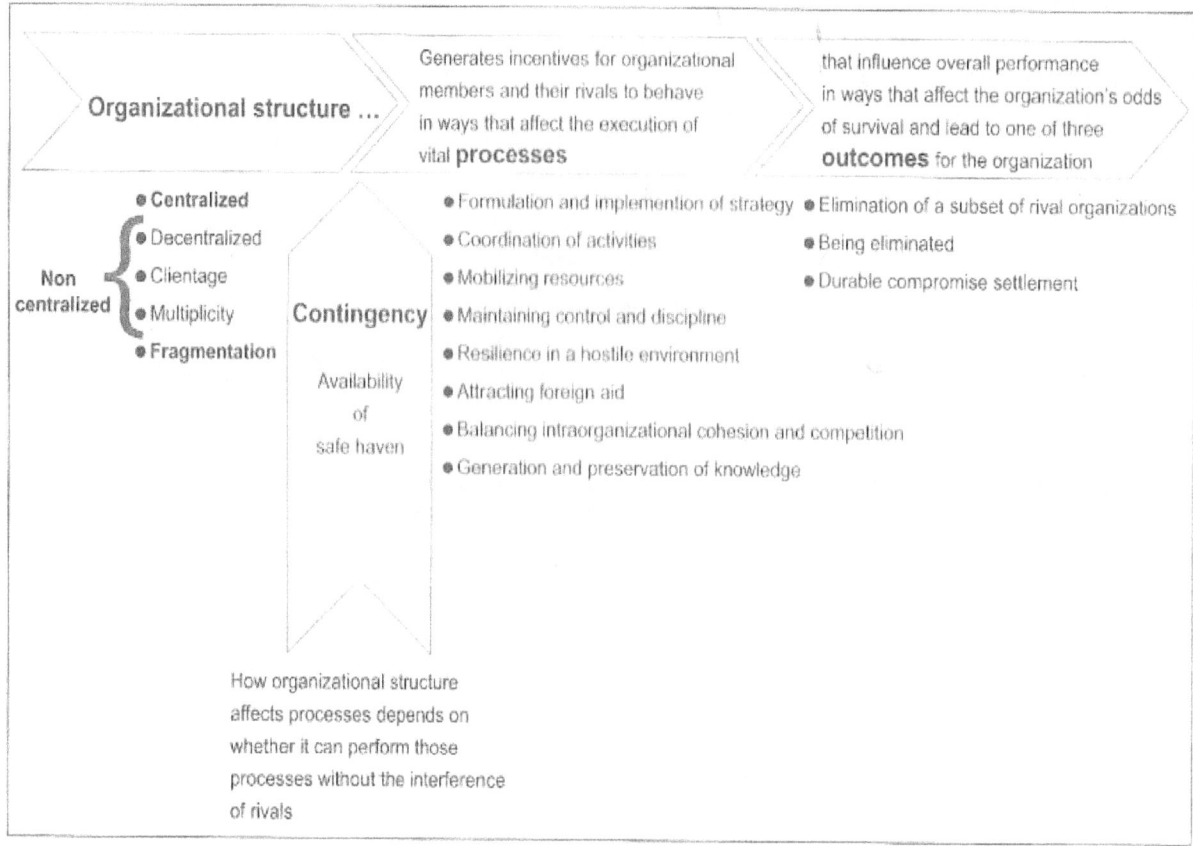

FIGURE 1.1.   Framework of the organizational theory of group conflict

Processes	Organizational structure									
	Centralization		Decentralization		Patronage		Multiplicity		Fragmentation	
Strategy	+	−	−	+	−	+	−	+	−	−
Coordination	+	+	−	+	+	+	+	−	~	−
Mobilization of resources	+	−	0	+	~	+	−	+	−	−
Control and discipline	+	+	−	+	+	+	+	+	−	−
Resilience	+	−	~	+	−	+	−	+	~	−
Foreign Aid	+	0	0	+	+	+	+	+	−	~
Intraorganiz- ational cohesion and competition	+	+	−	−	+	+	+	−	0	0
Generation and preservation of knowledge	+	~	−	+	−	+	~	+	−	−
Total Score	+8	-1	-6	+6	0	+8	0	+4	-7	-7

Key:
+ Organizational structure allows good performance of process
0 Structure is irrelevant or has little effect on process
− Structure impedes execution of process

(With safe haven / No safe haven)

Which simplifies to...

	Centralization	Patronage, Multiplicity, or Decentralization	Fragmentation
Safe haven	Good Fit	Bad Fit	Bad Fit
No safe haven	Bad Fit	Good Fit	Bad Fit

FIGURE 4.1. How structure influences organizational processes in territorial conflicts

APPENDIX D
COMISAF COIN Guidance

NATO / ISAF UNCLASSIFIED RELEASABLE TO GIRoA

Headquarters
International Security Assistance Force

Kabul, Afghanistan

08 September 2010

COMISAF/CDR USFOR-A

For the Commanders, Contracting Personnel, Military Personnel, and Civilians of NATO ISAF and US Forces-Afghanistan

SUBJECT: COMISAF's Counterinsurgency (COIN) Contracting Guidance

The scale of our contracting efforts in Afghanistan represents both an opportunity and a danger. With proper oversight, contracting can spur economic development and support the Afghan government's and ISAF's campaign objectives. If, however, we spend large quantities of international contracting funds quickly and with insufficient oversight, it is likely that some of those funds will unintentionally fuel corruption, finance insurgent organizations, strengthen criminal patronage networks, and undermine our efforts in Afghanistan.

In view of these points, contracting has to be "Commander's business." Indeed, I expect Commanders to consider the effects of our contract spending and understand who benefits from it. We must use intelligence to inform our contracting and ensure those with whom we contract work for the best interests of the Afghan people. We must be better buyers and buy from better people. Consistent with NATO and national contracting laws and regulations, we must:

Understand the role of contracting in COIN. Purchases we make for construction, goods, and services can bolster economic growth, stability, and Afghan goodwill toward their government and ISAF. Contracts with Afghan firms that procure Afghan goods and services generate employment and assist in the development of a sustainable economy. However, if we contract with powerbrokers who exclude those outside their narrow patronage networks or are perceived as funneling resources to one community at the expense of another, the effect on Afghan perceptions and our mission will be negative. Thus, we must incorporate COIN Contracting topics into training for Commanders.

Hire Afghans first, buy Afghan products, and build Afghan capacity. Use contracting to hire Afghan workers and Afghan-owned companies. If we are unable to contract with an Afghan company, encourage companies to hire Afghans and sub-contract with responsible Afghan firms. Emulate successes such as NTM-A/CSTC-A's Afghan First program that created a boot making industry in Kabul. Find solutions that tap existing, but sometimes limited, Afghan capacity, such as maximizing the opportunities for local small and medium-sized companies to compete for our contracts. Adapt procedures, such as facilitating base access, to remove obstacles to hiring Afghans. Wherever appropriate, use in-country sourcing rather than imports. Look for opportunities to incorporate maintenance and repair training in existing contracts to build Afghan skills and to create long-term employment. Focus efforts on promoting industries with immediate and long-term growth potential, such as agriculture, food processing, beverages, and construction. Adopt a fair wage and fair price approach that minimizes market shock and inflation. Guard against "front businesses" that fraudulently claim to be Afghan-owned.

Know those with whom we are contracting. Where our money goes is as important as the service provided or the product delivered. Establish systems and standard databases for vetting vendors and contractors to ensure that contracting does not empower the wrong people or allow the diversion of funds. Support contracting agencies and officers so they can get out in the field and build relationships with local businesses and community leaders. Gain and maintain visibility of the sub-contractor network. Contract with vendors that have fewer sub-contractors. Excessive sub-contracting tiers provide opportunities for criminal networks and insurgents to divert contract money from its intended purpose. Hold prime contractors responsible for the behavior and performance of their sub-contractors. Ensure that prime contractors provide detailed information on all sub-contractors consistent with coalition requirements and with CENTCOM Contracting Command's new sub-contractor clause.

Exercise responsible contracting practices. While we all desire fast results, haste in contracting invites fraud, waste, and abuse. Plan ahead, establish reasonable timelines, and ensure transparency and oversight so that contracting and procurement reinforce rather than detract from our objectives.

Integrate contracting into intelligence, plans, and operations. Commanders must know what contracting activity is occurring in their battlespace and who benefits from those contracts. Integrate contracting into intelligence, plans, and operations to exert positive influence and to better accomplish our campaign objectives. Commanders should use COIN Contracting Management Boards to coordinate contracting efforts and ensure contracts support campaign goals. Commanders and contracting agencies should share best practices, align policies and procedures, and exchange information on contractor performance—positive or negative (using digitally linked CIDNE/INDURE databases).

Consult and involve local leaders. Use local shuras and Afghan government and private sector leaders to prioritize projects, identify viable companies, vet potential contractors, improve oversight, hold contractors accountable, and provide post-award feedback to inform future projects. Work with and through the Ministry of Rural Reconstruction and Development to leverage existing monitoring, procurement, and implementation capabilities and to build long-term Afghan institutional capacity.

Develop new partnerships. Contracts with a broader range of Afghan companies will help break monopolies and weaken patronage networks that breed resentment. In situations where there is no alternative to powerbrokers with links to criminal networks, it may be preferable to forgo the project. Broadly advertise contract opportunities to local communities beyond bases. When appropriate, use NGOs to identify potential contracting partners and train them to navigate our contracting processes.

Look beyond cost, schedule, and performance. Evaluate the success of a contract by the degree to which it supports the Afghan people and our campaign objectives. Include operational criteria in decisions to award contracts such as the effect of the contract on security, local power dynamics, and the enemy.

Invest in oversight and enforce contract requirements. Ensure post-award oversight of contractors and their performance to get what we pay for and to ensure the contract supports our mission. Because the number of contracts each contracting officer oversees has increased, commands must devote additional personnel to oversight. Designate top-performers to serve as Contract Officer Representatives and ensure that they are trained and understand the operational importance of contracting.

Act. Upon identification of linkages between contractors and criminal networks, we must take appropriate actions, such as: suspension and debarment of the individuals or the company, contract termination, or not renewing a contract option period. Recognize that some of these actions may have broad or significant ramifications and plan accordingly. Establish rapid, flexible, and thorough processes to develop, coordinate, approve, and implement contract actions to end contracts that undermine our mission.

Get the story out. We must improve our contracting practices to ensure they fully support our mission. However, we must also recognize what our contracting has accomplished. Our contracting efforts have sustained widely dispersed and high tempo operations and helped build Afghan national security capacity. Our contracting has also improved the lives of many Afghans, enhanced infrastructure, delivered essential services, supported local businesses, increased employment, and fostered economic development.

David H. Petraeus
General, United States Army
Commander, International Security Assistance
Force/United States Forces-Afghanistan

APPENDIX E
Somalia Map

BIBLIOGRAPHY

Addario, Lynsey. "Veiled Rebellion," *National Geographic* (December 2010): 48-53.

Anonymous. *Through our Enemies' Eyes: Osama bin Laden*, Radical Islam, and the Future of America (Washington, DC: Brassey's Inc, 2002), 155.

Associated Press. "Oregon Bomb Suspect Wanted 'Spectacular Show," (Portland) http://www.msnbc.msn.com/id/40390013 (accessed November, 28 2010).

Biddle, Stephen. "The New U.S. Army/Marine Corps Counterinsurgency Field Manual as Political Science and Political Praxis," *Review Symposium*, Volume 6, No. 2 (June 2008): 348-351.

Blau,Thomas and Liskey, Daryl. "Analytics and Action in Afghanistan," *Prism*, Volume 1, No. 4 (September 2010): 41-56.

Blood, Peter. *Afghanistan: A Country Study* (Washington: GPO for the Library of Congress, 2001) http://countriestudies.us/afghanistan/57.htm (accessed 14 October, 2010).

Brown, Michael E. *Grave New World*. Washington, DC: Georgetown University Press, 2003.

Centers for Disease Control and Prevention, "Overview of Somali Culture," http://www.cdc.gov/tb/publications/guidestoolkits/EthnographicGuides/Somalia/default.htm (accessed January 7, 2011).

Central Intelligence Agency World Factbook, "South Asia: Afghanistan," https://www.cia.gov/library/publications/the-world-factbook/geos/af.html (accessed September 9, 2010).

Galula, David. *Counterinsurgency Warfare: Theory and Practice*. New York: Frederick A. Praeger Inc., 1964.

Gant, Jim. "One Tribe at a Time: A Strategy for Success in Afghanistan," Steven Pressfield Online, the Warrior Ethos, entry posted September 29, 2009, http://blog.stevenpressfield.com, (accessed on November 12, 2010).

Gentile, Gian P. "Freeing the Army from the Counterinsurgency Straitjacket," *The Joint Forces Quarterly*, Issue 58 (3rd Quarter, 2010).

Gentile, Gian P. "Time for the Deconstruction of Field Manual 3-24," *Joint Forces Quarterly*, Issue 58 (3rd Quarter, 2010).

Griffith, Samuel B. *Sun Tzu: The Art of War,* (New York: Oxford University Press, 1962), 50.

Hoffman, Bruce. *Inside Terrorism*, New York: Columbia University Press, 2006

Hoffman, Frank G. "Neo-Classical Counterinsurgency?," *Parameters* (Summer 2007).

Hunttington, Samuel P. *The Clash of Civilization and the Remaking of the World Order*, New York: Simon and Schuster, 1996.

iCasualties.org, http://icasuatlies.org/oef (accessed on 2 January, 2011).

Jackson, Alexander. "Operation Moshtarak: Lessons Learned," International Council on Security and Development, http://www.icosgroup.net/modules/reports/operation _moshtarak (accessed December 4, 2010).

Kagan, Frederick and Kagan, Kimberly. "Defining Success in Afghanistan," A Report by the American Enterprise Institute and the Institute for the Study of War, 2011.

Kilcullen, David. "Countering Global Insurgency," The Journal of Strategic Studies, Volume 28, No. 4 (August 2005).

Kilcullen, David. *The Accidental Guerilla*. New York: Oxford University Press, 2009.

Kim, Jiyul. "Cultural Dimensions of Strategy and Policy," Strategic Studies Institute, 2008.

Kimberlin, Joanne. "New Weapon in an Old War," *The Virginian-Pilot*, September, 26, 2010.

Larson, Dennis. "Somali Pirates: A New Phase Zero Stability Operational Approach , A Strategic Imperative in the Horn of Africa, " Joint Forces Staff College, 18 June 2010.

Mckelvey, Tara. "The Cult of Counterinsurgency," *The American Prospect*. http://www.prospect.org/cs/articles?article=the_cult_of_counterinsurgency (accessed September, 30, 2010).

Melshen, Paul. "Mapping Out a Counterinsurgency Campaign Plan: Critical Considerations in Counterinsurgency Campaigning," *Small Wars and Insurgencies*, Volume 18, No. 4 (December 2007): 667.

Memon, Ali Nawaz. "*Pashtunwali* Code of conduct for Pashtuns," Sindh Development Institute, entry posted February 13, 2008, http://sindhdi.wordpress.com/2008/02/13/*Pashtunwali*-code-of-conduct-of-pashtuns/ (accessed November 2, 2010).

Meredith, Kevin and Villarreal, Sergio, and Wilkinson, Mitchel, "Afghanistan: The De-evolution of Insurgency," *Small War Journal* (October 7, 2010): 10.

Metz, Steven. "Rethinking Insurgency." Strategic Studies Institute. http://www.StrategicStudiesInstitute.army.mil (accessed August 13, 2010).

Nagl, John A. "Constructing the Legacy of Field Manual 3-24," *Joint Forces Quarterly*, Issue 58, (3rd Quarter 2010).

Nagl, John. "Learning to Adapt and Win", *Joint Forces Quarterly*, Issue 58, (3rd Quarter 2010).

Nagl, John. *Learning to Eat Soup with a Knife*. Chicago: University of Chicago Press, 2002.

Nakamura, David. 2010. U.S. troop deaths in Afghan war up sharply. *The Washington Post*. September 1.

National Intelligence Council. *Global Trends 2025: A Transformed World*, GPO, Washington DC, November 2008.

Nouri, Khalil and Green, Terry. "Afghanistan Needs a Tribal Business Czar to Work with the U.S.," http://www.usborderfirereport.com/afghanistan_needs _a_tribal_busin.htm (Assessed on November 13, 2010).

Obama, Barrack. "Obama Remarks on Uganda, African Terroism," President Obama interview by the South African Broadcasting Corporation, July 13, 2010 (accessed from InsideDefense.Com on December 17, 2010).

Pashtunwali" in Afghan Roma Web Portal, https://ronna-afghan.harmonieweb.org/Pages/*Pashtunwali*.aspx, (accessed 5 November, 2010).

Perry, Tony. "Buckling Down in Helmand, Marines are thinking long-haul for fight for the Afghan province," *The Los Angeles Times*, August 28, 2010.

Peters, Ralph. "New Counterinsurgency Manual Cheats on the History Exam*," Armed Forces Journal International*, Issue 144 (February 2007).

Public Broadcasting Service, "Behind Taliban Lines," http://www.pbs.org/wgbh/pages/frontline/talibanlines/map/ (accessed November 12, 2010).

Rader, Ingrid. "Shaping the Information Environment in Afghanistan," *Small Wars Journal*, July 2010, http://smallwarsjournal.com (accessed on August 15, 2010).

Regehr, Ernie. "Reintegration and reconciliation in Afghanistan: In what order and at what price?" *The Ploughshares Monitor* (Spring 2010).

Ricks, Tom. *Fiasco*. New York: The Penguin Press, 2006.

Ronfeldt, David. *In Search of How Societies Work: Tribes the First and Forever Form, Rand* (Santa Monica, CA: Rand Corporation, (December 2006): 59.

Rodgers, Clifford J, "Clausewitz, Genius and the Rules," *The Journal of Military History* 66 (October 2002): 1167-1176.

Sinno, Abdulkader, H. *Organizations at War in Afghanistan and Beyond.* Ithaca and London: Cornell University Press, 2008.

Schrecker, Mark. "U.S. Strategy in Afghanistan: Flawed Assumptions Will Lead to Ultimate Failure," *Joint Forces Quarterly*, Issue 59 (4th Quarter 2010).

Smith, Neil. "Understanding Sri Lanka's Defeat of the Tamil Tigers," *Joint Forces Quarterly*, Issue 59 (4th Quarter 2010).

STRATFOR, "Limited Cooperation Between Somali Militants, Jemeni Jihadists," http://www.stratfor.com/analysis/20101209-limited-cooperation-between-somali-militants-yemini -jihadists (Accessed December 17, 2010).

Straziuso, Jason and Hassan, Mohamed Olad. "Hard-line rulers in Somalia take cues from the Taliban," *The Virginia Pilot.* August 22, 2010.

Taarnby, Michael and Hallundbaek, Lars, "Somalia: The Internalization of Militant Islam and the Implications for Radicalisation Processes in Europe," http://www.justitsministeriet.dk/fileadmin/downloads/Forskning_og_dokumentation/ Forskningspulje/Taarnby-rapport.pdf (accessed January 9, 2011).

The Fund for Peace, "Failed States Index 2010," http://www.fundforpeace.org/web/index.php?option=com_content&task=view&id=99&Itemid=140 (accessed on January 6, 2011).

Toft, Monica Duffy. "Getting Religion," *International Security*, Vol. 31, No. 4 (Spring 2007).

UNAMA, "Afghanistan: Annual Report on Protection of Civilians in Armed Conflict," (http://unama.unmissions.org/Portals/UNAMA/human%20rights/Protection%20of% 20Civilian%202009%20report%20English.pdf) (accessed on November 19, 2010).

U.S. Department of the Army. *Field Manual 3-24 Counterinsurgency,* GPO, Washington DC, 15 December 2006

U.S. Government. (2010) *National Security Strategy .* Washington: GPO, May 2010.

United States Department of State, "Somalia: Report on Female Genital Mutilation (FGM) or Female Genital Cutting (FGC)," http://www.state.gov/g/wi/rls/rep/crfgm/10109pf.htm (assessed January 9, 2011)

Watson, Jeff. "Language and Culture Training: Separate Paths?," *Military Review*, (March-April, 2010): 93-95.

BIOGRAPHY

COL Steven A. Baker (USA)
Most recently served as the Director of the Combined Joint Operations Center for the ISAF Joint Command in Kabul Afghanistan.

COL Baker was commissioned in 1988 at the United States Military Academy. Following initial training at Ft Belvior, VA as an engineer officer, he was assigned to a mechanized engineer battalion in Germany as a Platoon Leader, Executive Officer and Operations Officer. After supporting Operation DESERT STORM, he went on to command a line airborne engineer company and the Advanced Airborne School in the 82nd Airborne Division. Later he served with the US Army Corps of Engineers as a Resident Engineer and Operations Officer in New Jersey, Macedonia, Kosovo and Greenland. He returned to the 82nd Airborne Division as a Battalion Executive Officer, Assistant Division Engineer and he deployed to Afghanistan in 2003 to become the CTF-82, C-7. After a tour to NORTHCOM and JTF-N as the Chief of Tunnel Detection Operations, COL Baker was chosen for Battalion Command and returned to the 82nd Airborne and again deployed to Afghanistan where he led Task Force Diablo in combat operations in Paktia, Logar and Wardak Provinces as a Battle Space Owner for the 4th Brigade Combat Team. Upon his return, he took over as the Deputy Brigade Commander for the 20th Engineer Brigade (Airborne) until he was selected to assist in the standup of the ISAF Joint Command in Kabul.

COL Baker earned his Bachelor's Degree from the United States Military Academy. He later earned a Master's Degree in Civil Engineering from the University of Florida. Additionally, COL Baker is a graduate of the Army Command and General Staff Course, as well as the Joint Combined Warfighting School.

www.ingramcontent.com/pod-product-compliance
Lightning Source LLC
Chambersburg PA
CBHW081845280526
45789CB00007B/2572